A.T.Q. STEWART was born in Belfast, where he was educated at the Royal Belfast Academical Institution and Queen's University. After some years in teaching, he returned to Queen's as a lecturer, and was appointed Reader in Irish History in 1975. He took early retirement in 1990 to devote more time to writing, and he is a frequent broadcaster on radio and television. He was consultant to both BBC Television's *The History of Ireland* and Thames Television's *The Troubles* and was a presenter for the Channel 4 series *The Divided Kingdom*. Since 1970 he has contributed to many encyclopedias and works of reference, prepared sets of questions for the BBC *Mastermind* series, and written articles for newspapers and journals, including the *Spectator*, the *Irish Arts Review*, *History Ireland*, the *Irish Times*, *Irish Independent*, *Sunday Tribune* and the *Belfast Telegraph*. His publications include *The Ulster Crisis: Resistance to Home Rule, 1912–14* (Faber and Faber, 1967; reissued by Blackstaff Press, 1997), *The Pagoda War: Lord Dufferin and the Fall of the Kingdom of Ava* (Faber and Faber, 1972), *The Narrow Ground: Aspects of Ulster 1609–1969* (Faber and Faber, 1977; reissued by Blackstaff Press, 1997), *Edward Carson* (Gill and Macmillan, 1982; reissued by Blackstaff Press, 1997), *A Deeper Silence: The Hidden Origins of the United Irishmen* (Faber and Faber, 1993) and *The Summer Soldiers: The 1798 Rebellion in Antrim and Down* (Blackstaff Press, 1995). In 1977 he was a joint winner of the first Christoper Ewart-Biggs Memorial Prize for *The Narrow Ground*. He is married with two sons and lives in Belfast.

MICHAEL COLLINS

The Secret File
edited by A.T.Q. Stewart

PUBLIC RECORD OFFICE

THE
BLACKSTAFF
PRESS

BELFAST

First published in 1997 by
The Blackstaff Press Limited
3 Galway Park, Dundonald, Belfast BT16 0AN, Northern Ireland
in association with the
Public Record Office

Typeset by Techniset Typesetters, Newton-le-Willows, Merseyside

Printed in Northern Ireland by W. & G. Baird Limited

A CIP catalogue record for this book
is available from the British Library

ISBN 0-85640-614-7

CONTENTS

PREFACE

The file on Michael Collins is now held at the Public Record Office, Kew, under the document reference CO 904/196. It may be seen by anyone who has obtained a reader's ticket, which is freely available to any person who can supply formal proof of identity. Originally closed for a hundred years, it was first opened to public inspection on 11 March 1996 under the Open Government Initiative. This initiative, the subject of a White Paper on Open Government in 1993, was based on the presumption that information should be released, unless there were compelling and substantive reasons of national interest to withhold it. Thereafter, the Foreign and Commonwealth Office (FCO), which had inherited this and other Royal Irish Constabulary files from the Dublin Castle administration, established a Special Review Team to review all previously retained FCO records, identify any continuing sensitivity and release as many papers as possible to the Public Record Office.

The only papers from the file not included here are some which relate solely to persons other than Collins, or which duplicate information already given, *pro forma* lists of questions to police about forthcoming meetings, and covering notes of no significant content.

Further information about services available to readers at the Public Record Office, Kew, Richmond, Surrey, TW9 4DU, and current hours of opening may be obtained from the Reader Services Department (tel. 0181 392 5200).

I am grateful to Roger Dixon of the Ulster Folk and Transport Museum for his work in carrying out the picture research for this book.

A.T.Q. STEWART
AUGUST, 1997

INTRODUCTION

Towards midnight on 7 April 1919 Michael Collins was smuggled into the headquarters of the Dublin Metropolitan Police in Brunswick (now Pearse) Street, and locked into the documents room by a police typist called Ned Broy. For good measure Collins brought with him a friend, Sean Nunan, whom he had met on the way, and they spent the next few hours reading through the 'G' Detective Division's most secret files on wanted persons, including Collins's own. It was an anxious night for Broy. At one point a window in the office was broken by a drunken soldier outside, and if the police had come to inspect the damage Collins would probably have been discovered. When he read, near the beginning of his file, that he came from a 'brainy' family in Cork, he burst out laughing, to Broy's alarm. But he left the building safely in the early morning, and giving no sign of the importance of what he had learned, appeared fresh and alert at a meeting of Dáil Éireann a few hours later.

Escapades like this, where those around him held their breath while he balanced everything on the edge of a card, created the Collins legend. He worked hard on it himself. With the advantages of audacity, a quick temper, intelligence, charm and the good looks of a matinée idol, he could scarcely have failed to become the kind of figure film makers like to transmute into myth. History is kind to patriots of his stamp – William Tell, Robin Hood, Che Guevara – and has few tears to shed for their enemies and victims. Yet even the most grotesque subversions of history cannot outdistance the true facts of the story, of a country boy who became the first urban guerrilla, laid the foundations of a state and then negotiated its independence, was chairman of its Provisional Government, then commander in chief of its armed forces when it was plunged into civil war – all this before dying at the hands of his fellow republicans at the age of thirty-one.

Michael Collins – 'intelligence, charm and the good looks of a matinée idol'

This file contains the police reports which Collins saw that April night in 1919. We know this because of the reference to the 'brainy' family

(Document 2, pp. 40–1). Characteristically, Collins bragged about it afterwards, putting Broy and others at risk. With hundreds of other police files, it was removed from Dublin Castle to London when the Irish Free State was established in 1922, and remained closed to public inspection until 1996. The file belonged to the Royal Irish Constabulary, Crime Special Branch, in Dublin Castle and not to the Dublin Metropolitan Police, who will presumably have had their own file on Collins. It does contain correspondence from the Dublin Metropolitan Police and material which will have been duplicated on the Dublin Metropolitan Police file.

The Ireland into which Collins was born in 1890 was reeling from the shock of the Parnell divorce scandal. The furious dispute it provoked was to split the Irish Parliamentary Party for a generation. Yet only four years earlier these MPs, under Parnell's leadership, had seemed to be on the brink of achieving Home Rule for Ireland. However, in 1886 Gladstone's Bill was defeated, and by 1891 Parnell was dead. In the aftermath, with the prospect of Home Rule further receding, the parliamentary party was faced with a kind of cultural challenge. New cultural movements were converging, some of which accentuated the antipathies between the greater part of the island and the largely Protestant north-east, and in the end they changed the framework in which the Irish Question was to be debated.

At this time technological progress and commercial enterprise tended to emphasise, particularly in rural areas, the extent to which Ireland was becoming more anglicised. In response the Gaelic Athletic Association (GAA) was founded in 1884 to encourage Irish sports such as hurling. Under its patron, Dr Thomas William Croke, Archbishop of Cashel, it banned 'such foreign and fantastic field-sports as lawn tennis, polo, croquet, cricket and the like'. Another organisation which aimed at the 'de-Anglicisation' of Ireland was the Gaelic League. Founded by Douglas Hyde, the son of a Church of Ireland clergyman, it was devoted to the revival of the Irish language. Hyde was not concerned about political independence, and strove hard to keep politics out of his society, but it was inevitable that nationalists should be drawn to such cultural movements.

Among the political groups most supportive of these trends were those minority societies of extremists who looked back to the United Irishmen of 1798 for inspiration. For them 1898 was a significant anniversary. In that year Arthur Griffith, a Dublin printer who had spent some years in South Africa, launched a weekly paper, the *United Irishman*, to propagate his theory of independence, a doctrine which became known by the Irish title *Sinn Féin* – 'Ourselves'. Griffith did not believe that freedom could be won either by the efforts of Irish MPs at Westminster or by violent revolution.

Instead, drawing his inspiration from the Hungarian nationalist Francis Deák, and the dual monarchy of the Austro-Hungarian Empire, he advocated that elected representatives should refuse to take their seats in parliament, and eventually create a government in Ireland. This would have the moral authority to rule, and would oblige the British to withdraw peacefully.

All these movements were watched from the shadows by the Irish Republican Brotherhood (IRB), a secret, oath-bound, republican society surviving from the days of the Fenian uprising in 1867. Its members were sworn to free Ireland through violent revolution, and to set up an independent republic on the model projected by Wolfe Tone in 1798. They had powerful support, especially financial support, from the Clan na Gael organisation of Irish-Americans in the United States. The IRB was responsible for the dynamite outrages in England in the 1880s (for which Tom Clarke was sentenced to penal servitude for life) but they had little support among the Irish population as a whole, which placed its hopes of achieving Home Rule on its representatives in parliament.

There were three attempts between 1885 and 1914 to give Ireland autonomy by parliamentary and democratic means. William Gladstone's first Home Rule Bill was defeated in the House of Commons in 1886. His second Home Rule Bill passed the Commons in 1892, but was defeated in the House of Lords. For the next two decades Home Rule was, in Tim Healy's phrase, put 'into cold storage'. When the Liberals returned to power in a landslide victory in the election of 1906, they could afford virtually to ignore Irish grievances until 1910. The two elections of that year (one consequent on the death of King Edward VII) strengthened the influence of the Irish Parliamentary Party, now reunited under the leadership of John Redmond after the bitter divisions following the Parnell divorce scandal of 1890. Herbert Asquith's government was persuaded to introduce a third Home Rule Bill, and this time its passage seemed assured because of the changes the Liberals had made to the Constitution. By the Parliament Act of 1911, the House of Lords could no longer hold up legislation for more than three parliamentary sessions.

However, a grave constitutional crisis was created when the Conservative opposition took the issue outside parliament, and mobilised Unionist opinion throughout Great Britain and Ireland to defeat the Bill by any means short of insurrection. The Conservatives, led by Andrew Bonar Law, had several advantages in the dispute, not least their virtual control of the press and the overt sympathy of the officer class in the British armed services, but their strongest card was the absolute determination of the majority Protestant population of north-east Ireland to resist the implementation of Home Rule, by force of arms if necessary. Under the leadership of Sir Edward Carson and Captain James Craig, the Unionists raised an Ulster Volunteer Force (UVF) of one hundred thousand men, and in April 1914 defied the authorities by landing twenty-five thousand German and Italian rifles at Larne, County Antrim, and elsewhere. The Royal Navy sent warships to Belfast Lough, and the army was put on standby, but in the end, partly because officers stationed at the Curragh camp in County Kildare were offered the option of not serving in Ulster and promptly took it (it was hardly a 'mutiny' as such), the operation against the UVF was abandoned. In spite of this, the Government of Ireland Bill (to give it its proper name) duly passed through all the necessary stages in parliament and became law on 18 September 1914. By then, however, Britain had been at war with Germany for seven weeks, and the operation of the Act was suspended for the duration of hostilities.

After Patrick Pearse complained that the Orangeman with a rifle was a less ridiculous figure than the nationalist without one, a citizen army of Volunteers was raised in the south, on similar lines to the UVF. The Gaelic League provided the leadership, and the chosen head of the movement was Eoin MacNeill, professor of early Irish history at University College Dublin. The raising of the Volunteers was a serious embarrassment to Redmond, but he was reluctantly obliged to give them his blessing. They were not embodied in order to fight the Ulster Volunteers, but to emulate them in intimidating the British government. Nevertheless Ireland had seemed to be drifting towards a civil war when the European crisis intervened.

Since Britain had gone to war ostensibly in defence of Belgium, a small country whose population was Catholic, Redmond urged recruitment to the British Army among the Volunteers, as Carson had among the Ulstermen. This made Redmond highly unpopular with the various separatist groups, and in particular with the IRB, which had involved itself clandestinely in the raising of the Volunteers in hopes of using them for its own political ends. The Volunteers split, and a minority of 11,000 out of the 180,000 total formed a separate force, with MacNeill as chief of staff. They took the name of the Irish Volunteers, while the majority continued to be known as the National Volunteers.

Another paramilitary organisation, the Irish Citizen Army, had arisen from labour troubles in Dublin in 1913, when the police clashed violently with strikers. It was led by James Connolly, a trade unionist of Marxist opinions. In spite of his internationalist views, Connolly was an ardent Irish patriot, who came to believe that independence was the first step to

The Royal Irish Constabulary, *c.* 1916 – 'a semi-military force, armed and drilled'

socialist revolution. He therefore joined the IRB in their plan of insurrection.

The whole climate of opinion in Ireland was changed by the unexpected outbreak of the Easter Rising in Dublin in 1916. Though most people deplored it at the time as an act of reckless and hopeless folly, a betrayal of the thousands of nationalists who were fighting in France, it soon came to be invested with certain glamour, especially after the execution by firing squad of fifteen of the rebel leaders. They were, for the most part, idealists, and their action was seen as a symbolic sacrifice by a resurgent Irish nation that was determined to be free. The Rising had been carefully planned by the IRB, and the survivors of 1916, when they were eventually released from prison, were destined to become the leaders of the new nationalism in Ireland.

There were two separate police forces in Ireland in 1916, the Royal Irish Constabulary and the Dublin Metropolitan Police. The first recognisably modern body of police in Ireland dated from the period of Sir Robert Peel's chief secretaryship (1812–18), whence they derived their colloquial name of 'peelers', but it was really Drummond's Act of 1836 (called after the under-secretary in Lord Melbourne's government) which laid the foundations of the Irish constabulary. Repealing all previous legislation, it consolidated and placed under central control the entire police of the country, except for the city of Dublin. The lord lieutenant was empowered to appoint an inspector general of police 'who shall reside in Dublin and shall be charged and invested with the general Direction and Superintendence of the Force to be established under this Act'. He was to be assisted by county inspectors and sub-inspectors, and for every city or town (except Dublin) 'a Chief Constable, two Head Constables and such constables as might be required for the preservation of the Peace therein'.

Applicants for the post of police officer were to be under the age of forty, fit and able-bodied, and able to read and write. They had to be of good character, possessing qualities of 'honesty, fidelity and activity'. Gamekeepers, tithe collectors, owners of public houses, and certain other occupations, were ineligible. Every policeman had to take an oath faithfully to serve the sovereign and to keep the peace, and not to join any political or secret society 'unless the Society of Freemasons'. In 1867 the force was renamed the Royal Irish Constabulary (RIC) by Queen Victoria, in recognition of the loyal service they had shown during the Fenian Rising of that year.

This recognition emphasised the one vital respect in which the RIC differed from police forces elsewhere in the United Kingdom. From the very beginning, it had semi-military duties to perform. As the *Morning Post* tried to explain for puzzled English readers in 1920, 'crisis after crisis has brought them into collision with a brave and excitable populace . . . It is no wonder, then, that the RIC is a semi-military force, armed and drilled, and concentrated in those little barrack forts that are the blockhouses of Imperial rule in Ireland.'

The Dublin Metropolitan Police; a separate, unarmed force whose jurisdiction included the city of Dublin, Blackrock, Dalkey, Kingstown, Pembroke and Rathmines.

The capital city of Dublin had been specifically excluded from Drummond's Act. A separate Act, passed in the same year, provided a police force for Dublin and the metropolitan area. The city, along with part of the county of Dublin, was divided into six sections, each in the charge of a superintendent of police. The Dublin Metropolitan Police (DMP) had a constant strength of just over a thousand men, and were paid for partly out of the city rates. The six divisions of the DMP were designated by letters of the alphabet, A to F. A seventh detective division, G, dealt with serious crime, both ordinary and political, and was therefore responsible for the surveillance of political suspects and subversive movements.

Michael Collins was born at Woodfield, his family's ninety-acre farm near Clonakilty in County Cork, on 18 October 1890, the youngest of eight children. His father, born in the year of Waterloo, was seventy-five, his mother, née Mary Anne O'Brien, was thirty-five. His eldest brother, John, took over the farm on their father's death six and a half years later, and Michael continued to live there until he was sixteen, when he took up a job in the Post Office Savings Bank in London. Here he lived at 5 Netherwood Place, Kensington, with his sister Johanna (Hannie), who was also a Post Office employee. Like most Irish people in England they mixed mainly with their compatriots rather than assimilating into English society, and the cultural influences Michael was exposed to were largely Irish. 'I had Irish friends in London before I arrived,' he wrote later, 'and in the intervening years I had made more friends among Irish residents in London. For the most part we lived lives apart. We chose to consider ourselves outposts of our nation.'

This was the classic recipe for a revolutionary nationalist, and Collins belonged precisely to the generation of young people most affected by the new forces at work in Irish society. His national school education in Ireland had steeped him in the history of Irish revolutions, 'old, unhappy, far-off things and battles long ago'. He shared the enthusiasm for a Gaelic past and the Irish language, which he always found difficult to master, though his parents had been native Irish speakers. A natural athlete, he enjoyed all physical sports, especially football and hurling, and was a very active member of the GAA, becoming secretary of his London club, the Geraldines. The GAA was a recruiting ground for the IRB. Through a Cork friend, Sam Maguire, who also worked in the Post Office in London, Collins was sworn in as an IRB member in 1909, and later was appointed treasurer of the South of England district. This decision determined the entire course of his short life.

In 1910 he left the Post Office to work briefly as a messenger in Horne and Company, a firm of stockbrokers, and then as a clerk in the Labour Exchange in Whitehall. When the war broke out, fearing that he might be conscripted, he contemplated moving to the United States, where one of his brothers lived, and took a post as clerk with the London office of the Guaranty Trust Company of New York. But at the beginning of 1916 he returned to Ireland, and immediately became involved in the IRB's plans for rebellion.

The General Post Office; burned out after the 1916 Rising

1916

The IRB's chosen instrument was to be the breakaway Irish Volunteers. Acting on the old adage that England's difficulty was Ireland's opportunity, and hoping to exploit the religious symbolism of Easter, they conspired to use the cover of the Volunteers' Easter Sunday exercises on 23 April 1916 to seize the main buildings in Dublin and proclaim an Irish Republic. The Volunteers' chief of staff, Eoin MacNeill, was kept in the dark until almost the last moment. Horrified when he discovered the truth, he immediately countermanded the order for mobilisation and wrecked the IRB's plans. Word was sent secretly to the Dublin battalions, however, and the rebellion went ahead on Easter Monday, with historic consequences.

The rebels, under the command of members of the IRB army council, occupied the General Post Office (GPO) and other key buildings in Dublin. Dublin Castle, and the military and police authorities, were taken by surprise. All police were withdrawn from the streets and the city's main thoroughfare was given over to widespread looting by the populace. For the first two days the men in the GPO waited for an attack which did not come. Then on Wednesday hastily brought-up field artillery and the guns of the warship *Helga*, stationed on the Liffey, began to rain shells on the GPO, setting it on fire. With the fire out of control, and no possibility of a successful sortie, Patrick Pearse surrendered unconditionally at four o'clock on Saturday afternoon.

Collins had left his lodgings at 16 Rathdown Road on Easter Monday morning, wearing a smart staff captain's Volunteer uniform, which was to cause some amusement among his comrades, and soon he was helping to break the windows of the GPO to provide firing points. 'Glory be to God!' exclaimed a woman passing in the street, 'would you look at them smashing all the lovely windows.' Pearse had earlier had to bear the indignity of his sister calling out to him, 'Come home, Patrick, and leave all this foolishness!'

One of the IRB's chosen military strategists was the poet Joseph Mary Plunkett, though he had no military experience

Joseph Mary Plunkett's brothers George and John (*left*) under arrest after the 1916 Rising

and was terminally ill with tuberculosis. Collins was his aide, and, on Good Friday, had in fact collected him from a nursing home where Plunkett was recovering from an operation on his throat. An eyewitness recorded Collins moving restlessly about the room while a nurse fixed Plunkett's bandages, before Collins took him to the Metropole Hotel. Accounts of Collins's demeanour in the GPO are sketchy and sometimes inconsistent. His first action was to pour a large quantity of porter into the drains, on the grounds that drink had done for the rebels of 1798. Thereafter he was in charge of the operations room under the parapeted roof of the GPO. When the fire took hold on Friday he worked frantically with a detail of men to hold it back with sand and water.

Pearse decided to try to occupy and fortify buildings in Great Britain Street, and The O'Rahilly and some of his men went to reconnoitre. Told at once that the positions were strongly held by British troops, Pearse countermanded the order and it was Collins who went after them, under fire. O'Rahilly was cut down, and so was Collins's friend from boyhood days, Seán Hurley. In *Michael Collins and the Invisible Army*, Desmond Ryan relates one account that speaks of Collins at the end sitting in a corner, 'a look of horror in his eyes, a pallor spreading over his face . . .'

The key to Collins's attitude in 1916 was his pragmatism. He did not hold a high opinion of Pearse, much preferring Connolly, and he thought well of Tom Clarke and Seán MacDermott. Desmond FitzGerald described Collins as 'the most active and efficient officer in the place', and his angry rebuke to a fellow-prisoner after the surrender says much: 'We lost, didn't we?'

After the surrender the prisoners were led away under military escort, through crowds of Dubliners who jeered and spat at them. On Sunday they were assembled at Richmond Barracks, where detectives from the DMP picked out and identified the ringleaders. Collins was one of those selected for further investigation, but, with a facility he was to display many times in the future, he managed to blend into the anonymous mass of the unrecognised rank and file. These prisoners were taken to England and placed in detention camps there. In June most of them were transferred to Frongoch, near Bala in north Wales. There Collins at once showed his practicality and flair for organisation, gaining in the process his famous nickname 'The Big Fellow'.

At Frongoch, Collins reconstituted a cell of the IRB, and men like Gearóid O'Sullivan, Richard Mulcahy, Terence MacSwiney and Tomás MacCurtain turned the camp into an academy of revolution. 'We set up our own university there,' one of them later observed, 'and from that camp came the hard core of the subsequent guerrilla war in Ireland.' When they learned that some of them, including Collins, might be liable for conscription, they began to confuse the camp's military guardians by

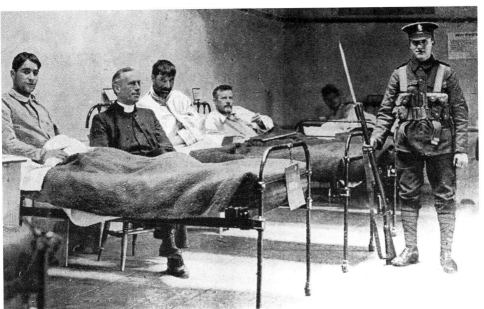

Wounded rebels from 1916 under guard in a temporary hospital set up in
Dublin Castle

giving the wrong names or no names at all, and were duly punished for
breach of prison rules.

Collins, encouraged by the fall of Asquith's coalition government, observed that he would not be surprised to find himself home for Christmas.
It was a prophetic remark. They had represented their loss of privileges so
tellingly to the outside world that questions were being asked in parliament, and the chief secretary announced an amnesty. On 21 December
the prisoners were assembled in the dining hall and told that they were to
be freed. The weary duty officer told them that he had to telegraph the
name and address of every man to the Home Office and Dublin Castle
before he left the camp that night. If they wanted to be home for Christmas, it was up to them. Collins and W.J. Brennan-Whitmore agreed to
draw up the list themselves, and a few hours later Collins was boarding
the steamer at Holyhead.

Collins reached home the day after Christmas. There was no one to
meet him at Clonakilty and he walked the four miles to Woodfield
through the chill December dark, only to learn on his arrival that his be-
loved grandmother, Mrs O'Brien, had just died, and that his brother John
and sister-in-law Katty were both ill. It was an abrupt anti-climax after the
euphoria of release, and he was not surprisingly depressed. 'I didn't feel at
all well,' he confided to an old sweetheart, Susan Killeen. 'Some kind of
reaction was setting in.' He was very disappointed at the attitude of the
country people. The war had made the local farmers too prosperous, and
they had become cautious in their politics. When he went into Clonakilty

with John he got into arguments, and he sensed that his presence caused unease.

1 9 1 7

Dublin Castle was in fact keeping track of the returned 1916 men and their activities through the DMP and the RIC, though not very efficiently. The detective department of the DMP noted on 8 January 1917 that Collins had not returned to the lodgings at 16 Rathdown Road, Dublin, which he had left on the fateful Easter Monday (Document 1, p. 39). From Cork the RIC duly reported that he had turned up at Clonakilty on 26 December, and had remained at Woodfield with his brother John. The county inspector was able to furnish Dublin with a description. 'He is a young man of fair complexion, clean shaven, strong jaws and features, may be 28 years of age. He belongs to a family [of] "brainy" people who are disloyal and of advanced Sinn Fein sympathies' (Document 2, pp. 40–1). It was this sentence which caused Collins so much amusement during his audacious visit to DMP headquarters in 1919.

The inspector general's annotation of the reports shows the extent to which the authorities underestimated Collins's importance as an IRB member. By mid-January 1917 he had moved to Sunday's Well, Cork, to live with his sister Mary, who was married to an excise officer called Powell (Documents 2 and 3, pp. 40–3). Not until 17 January did the DMP establish that the Michael Collins of Woodfield, of Sunday's Well, and of Dublin were one and the same (Document 4, p. 44). All the time he remained in his home county Collins had led 'what may be considered a retired life, and no notice was taken of his presence in the locality by anyone' (Document 6, pp. 46–7). Like the fictional Scarlet Pimpernel, he had an undoubted talent for always appearing to be the innocent bystander.

At the end of January 1917 Collins returned to Dublin and applied for the post of secretary of the Irish National Aid and Volunteers' Dependants' Fund. It had been created by the merger of two charities established after the rebellion to assist prisoners and their families. Irish National Aid had been set up by Dublin Corporation, and the Irish Republican Prisoners' Dependants' Fund by the widow of the veteran revolutionary Tom Clarke, executed for his part in the rebellion. Kathleen Clarke still had some of the gold sent by the American Clan na Gael to finance the rising, and she now used it for the dependants. Collins's youth and hasty temper caused him to be regarded with suspicion, and some of the committee thought him quite unsuitable. However, unknown to him, several of his

Frongoch friends were using their influence behind the scenes to secure his appointment, which was confirmed on 19 February (Document 7, p. 48). The release of so many of the prisoners by the spring of 1917 had increased the work involved, and Collins was paid two pounds and ten shillings a week.

The position gave Collins a greater standing in the various levels of the underground physical force movement, and enabled him to contact IRB members in all parts of the country. His efficiency in running the Aid Fund from its Dublin headquarters at 10 Exchequer Street was noted in national-ist circles (Document 7, p. 48), but Collins's ambitions were wider. He was at the same time active in helping to reorganise the Volunteers, the IRB itself and Griffith's Sinn Féin party, besides re-establishing strong links with Clan na Gael in the United States (Document 15, p. 58).

At this time Irish national-ist aspirations were mani-fested in many forms and through the agency of many organisations. The constitu-tional Irish Parliamentary Party in the British House of Commons still commanded the loyalty of most Catholic Irishmen and Irishwomen, though its continued failure to bring the ship of Irish Home Rule into harbour had undermined its authority. Griffith's minority Sinn Féin party still had its own slightly eccentric Austro-Hungarian model, which held that

Arthur Griffith with Collins: Collins did not want to be 'chalked up' as a supporter of Griffith's in 1916. Yet the careers of the two men were to be closely linked.

elected representatives should not sit at Westminster. (Griffith had op-posed the rising, but once it had begun he offered to join it on Easter Monday.) The separatists who adhered to the principles of the Fenians and the United Irishmen were at one on the need for violent revolution and the establishment of Wolfe Tone's Irish Republic, but were often divided on strategy.

The British soldiers involved in the fighting in Dublin at Easter 1916, and the English press, had referred to the rebels simply as 'Sinn Féiners' and the name stuck, though it was quite inaccurate. Griffith was not pleased, and Collins told his friends that he was disgusted to be 'chalked up' as a supporter of Griffith's. However, Sinn Féin was to prove the catalyst in what followed (Document 11, p. 51–2). The resurgence of Griffith's party began when it won a by-election in North Roscommon in February 1917. The astutely chosen candidate was George Plunkett, the elderly father of the three Plunkett brothers involved in the rising. Joseph Plunkett, to whom Collins had been aide in the GPO, had been executed, but his brothers had had their sentences commuted to ten years' penal servitude. George Plunkett was a poet, scholar, and Count of the Holy Roman Empire. Though not standing formally as a Sinn Féin candidate, he had the support of Sinn Féin and other groups, and he was returned by a comfortable majority.

When another by-election occurred in South Longford in April, Collins enthusiastically proposed as a candidate a local man, Joseph McGuinness, who was serving a sentence in Lewes jail. The idea met with considerable opposition. Arthur Griffith wanted to put forward his own Sinn Féin candidate, and an incensed Collins told him that Sinn Féin was 'balderdash' (meaning Griffith's dual monarchy theory). 'We want a Republic,' he said. Griffith silenced the truculent young man with a glacial stare, but, though 'a fanatic in his own right', he eventually gave way for the good of the wider cause. A more formidable obstacle was Eamon de Valera, another survivor of the Easter Rising, who had made himself spokesman for the Lewes prisoners. His chess-player's mind was working several moves ahead, and he feared the consequences to the movement as a whole if the Sinn Féin candidate were defeated, as seemed to him very likely. On his instructions, McGuinness refused to allow his name to go forward.

Collins ignored de Valera and went ahead anyway, adopting the ingenious slogan, 'Put him in to get him out'. He went to Granard in County Longford and threw himself heart and soul into the campaign which, as de Valera had predicted, was closely fought. On the first count Patrick McKenna, the Irish Parliamentary Party candidate, was elected by a narrow margin, but 'a bundle of uncounted votes was then discovered' and McGuinness was declared the winner by thirty-seven votes. Many years afterwards the respectable chairman of an Irish building society explained to Collins's biographer, Tim Pat Coogan, how the bundle was discovered. 'I jumped up on the platform, put a .45 to the head of the returning officer, clicked back the hammer, and told him to think again.'

During the campaign Collins and his friends stayed at the Greville Arms, a hotel owned by the Kiernan family, four attractive sisters and their brother. It was one of those all-purpose commercial enterprises which included, besides the hotel, a grocery and hardware shop, a bakery, and an undertaking and hire car business. Collins fell in love with one of the girls, Helen, but she eventually married Paul McGovern, a solicitor. On the night before her wedding he is said to have gone to the hotel and pleaded with her not to go through with the marriage. Later, however, he transferred his affections to her sister Kitty, with whom his friend Harry Boland was already in love. A third sister, Maud, was being courted by Thomas Ashe. Collins and Boland would later take opposite sides politically, and the fact that they were both in love with the same woman may have contributed to this. Kitty Kiernan became engaged to Collins in 1921. (After his death she married Felix Cronin, then quartermaster-general of the Irish Army, and died in 1945.) This involvement with the Kiernan family explains why Collins was in Granard so often at this time.

The year 1917 was one of continued electoral success for Sinn Féin. After his release from Lewes jail, de Valera changed his mind about strategy and contested the seat in East Clare left vacant by the death of Major Willie Redmond, the brother of the leader of the parliamentary party who had joined the Irish Guards at fifty-six, and died of wounds in France that June. De Valera won the seat easily on 11 July, polling 5,010 votes against the 2,035 of his nationalist opponent. There could be no question of intimidation this time, and when he returned to Dublin he was welcomed by a meeting attended by thousands of people. One of the speakers was Thomas Ashe, a fellow prisoner in Lewes, who said: 'We heard whispers in prison that a new Ireland had arisen, but we never dreamt anything like the reality we have seen.' A few weeks later, when the nationalist MP for Kilkenny died, the seat was taken for Sinn Féin by another ex-Lewes prisoner, William T. Cosgrave. In addition to these victories the Irish Parliamentary Party MP for Westmeath, Laurence Ginnell, defected to Sinn Féin. Ginnell, a barrister and a founder member of the Irish Literary Society, was to be appointed director of propaganda by Dáil Éireann in 1919 (Documents 11 and 12, pp. 51–3).

The problem for the British government was that after 1914 there seemed no possibility of coercing Protestant Ulster into accepting Home Rule. Partly to conciliate American opinion, since every effort was being made to bring the United States into the war, Prime Minister David Lloyd George made John Redmond an offer of immediate Home Rule, with the exclusion of the six counties of the north-east for five years. All such attempts to agree on exclusion had failed before 1914, and by now Redmond dared not even contemplate such a solution. As a compromise, he agreed to the calling of an Irish Convention, representing all sections of Irish opinion, to debate the question. It sat in Trinity College Dublin, under the chairmanship of Sir Horace Plunkett, from July 1917 until April

1918, but it was doomed from the outset; Sinn Féin refused to attend, and the northern Unionists would not yield on exclusion. Only the southern Unionists, whose situation seemed hopeless in any event, appeared disposed to compromise (Document 38, pp. 96–7).

During the summer of 1917 Collins and his chief associates were travelling about the country forming Sinn Féin clubs (Documents 19–23, pp. 62–71). The police were very interested in their movements, and particularly in the links which Dublin-based suspects were making with activists in the rural areas. Reports by the RIC inspectors were sent to the DMP and the Castle. At the end of July Collins is seen in County Longford in the company of Griffith and Ashe (Document 14, pp. 56–7). On 28 July Dublin Castle issued a proclamation prohibiting the carrying of arms in public places. In an attempt further to curb the Volunteers, more arms raids were carried out by the RIC and the military, and some of the ex-prisoners were arrested and sent to jail again for making seditious speeches. This was to happen to Ashe a few days later, with consequences no one could have foreseen.

In response to the growing disaffection in the country, the authorities

Sergeant Reidy with his family; his name appears on some of the Longford documents

began to make increased use of the stringent wartime regulations of the Defence of the Realm Act (DORA) which permitted trial of civilians by court martial for such offences as seditious speeches and illegal drilling. Among the close friends Collins made at this time was Thomas Ashe who was, after de Valera, the most senior of the 1916 rebel officers to have survived, and who had been elected head of the IRB. In August 1917 Ashe was arrested and charged with making a seditious speech at Ballinalee in County Longford. Collins, who had shared the platform with him at the meeting, visited him in the Curragh detention centre, and attended his court martial two weeks later. At this stage Collins treated the prosecution as a huge joke, telling Ashe's sister it was rather like Gilbert and Sullivan's *Trial By Jury*.

Two other Sinn Féin members, Austin Stack and Fionán Lynch, had been arrested on similar charges, and Ashe's sentence was the lightest of the three – one year's imprisonment. However, given the nature of the regulations under which they were tried, they protested at being treated as common criminals. By now there were about forty prisoners in Mountjoy jail convicted under the DORA legislation, and they began to organise themselves to demand special status as political prisoners. When they broke prison rules they were punished by having their boots and bedding removed, and they then went on hunger-strike. The authorities' response was forcible feeding, so inexpertly administered that on 25 September Ashe suddenly collapsed. He was taken to the Mater Misericordiae Hospital where he died a few hours later (Document 27, pp. 77–9).

The death of a prominent Volunteer in such circumstances was like a lighted match thrown on petrol. In accordance with a well-established tradition, his funeral became a vast organised demonstration of Irish nationalist protest, during which the Dublin Brigade of the Volunteers virtually took over the city. Sinn Féin had been given a propaganda weapon that they were able to use to enormous effect throughout the world, and particularly in the United States. Collins, in Volunteer uniform, delivered the graveside address, and afterwards was observed weeping bitterly.

On Sunday 7 October Collins returned

Sinn Féin!

A MONSTER

MEETING

WILL BE HELD AT

BALLINALEE

On Sunday, 7th October,

Under the Auspices of the North Longford Sinn Féin Executive. The following Speakers have promised to attend:—Messrs.

JOE McGUINNESS, M.P.,

Collins, Darrell Figgis, Francis McGuinness, and several Local Speakers.

COME IN YOUR THOUSANDS

And be convinced of the effectiveness of the Policy of Passive Resistance.

CHAIR TO BE TAKEN AT 3 O'CLOCK (IRISH TIME).

Go Mairidh ar nGaedhílg Slan.

to Ballinalee to speak at a meeting convened in Ashe's memory. 'In the circumstances I came out on the strong side,' he recorded, and not surprisingly there was 'a bit of unpleasantness with a policeman who was taking notes'. The policeman gave up his notes and there was no further trouble (Documents 24–9, pp. 72–84).

· Such meetings posed great practical difficulties for the RIC. If a constable attended and openly took notes, he was likely to become, as on this occasion, the object of hostility – and from people who were usually his neighbours. If a government shorthand note-taker was sent to the meeting, as Constable Byers observed, then a force of twenty policemen would have to come from another district to protect him. Most village police barracks were manned by a sergeant and two or three constables. One can sense Constable Byers's frustration. His sergeant is off-duty, 'sick', and he is obliged to furnish the necessary report to the district inspector (Document 25, pp. 73–4). If prosecutions were to stand up in court then the evidence of what had been said had to be reliable and, if possible, corroborated. The usual practice was therefore for two policemen to attend the meeting in plain clothes and make 'mental notes' which they then wrote up in the station.

Documents 27 and 28, pp. 77–83, are the 'mental notes' of Constable Joseph and the (presumably convalescent) Sergeant Casey. There are, as might be expected, minor discrepancies, but both are quite sure that Collins said, 'You will not get anything from the British Government unless you approach them with a bullock's tail in one hand and a landlord's head in the other', and this colourful sentence was duly marked 'A' for attention at a higher level, though no action was taken against Collins at this time (Document 28, pp. 80–3).

The Ballinalee meeting took place in a month which witnessed momentous decisions for the groups making up the nationalist movement. On 25 October 1917 the various separatist organisations united under the banner of Sinn Féin. De Valera was no longer connected with the IRB, but its members had decided to support him for the presidency of the whole movement. He also had the support of the Volunteers. When Griffith stood aside, accepting the post of vice-president, de Valera was duly elected. Two days later, at a separate convention, de Valera was elected president of the Volunteers, with Collins appointed as their director of organisation. De Valera had begun his extraordinary rise to power.

Outwardly unprepossessing, and totally lacking in the kind of panache displayed by Collins, de Valera had a diplomatist's gift for making irreconcilables appear to converge. His temperament was academic, and in different circumstances he might have been content to be a dry-as-dust professor. Astute, often enigmatic and cautious, he frequently irritated other nation-alists, especially Collins. He derived enormous prestige from the fact that he was the senior surviving commandant of 1916. He may have been saved from execution by the intervention of the United States consul, because he was American by birth, but this is not known for certain. This seniority gave him a certain control over republican militants like Collins, without committing him to accepting their methods. The one con-stant and clear factor in his make-up was his bitter hatred of England.

Arthur Griffith with Eamon de Valera; when Griffith stood aside, de Valera was elected president of Sinn Féin in October 1917

Collins threw himself into his new work as director of organisation with characteristic energy and efficiency, but the IRB had not succeeded in securing the key position of chief of staff of the Volunteers. That went to the stubborn and independent-minded Cathal Brugha. De Valera was very suspicious of the IRB members at this stage (two others had been appointed to key posts) and he thought that Collins was 'organising more than the Volunteers'.

1918

In March 1918, when the Volunteer executive again considered the ques-tion of who should be chief of staff, they showed their uneasiness about Collins's temperament by choosing Richard Mulcahy instead. Collins was appeased with the additional post of adjutant general. Despite the dis-trust shown by de Valera and Mulcahy, however, he was steadily in-creasing his influence in the Volunteer organisation, building the secret army that would become the first Irish Republican Army (IRA). As adjut-ant general he was placed in charge of discipline and training, but this was a role he already exercised, travelling about the country addressing meetings and, under the guise of 'Irish classes' and sports events, selecting the men who might be prepared to take up arms against the police and the British Army. The documents concerning incidents at Tullyvrane, County Longford, show him drilling recruits and conducting a Volunteer court martial just at this time (Documents 32–4, pp. 87–90).

In March 1918 the German army launched the Ludendorff offensive, its last and most dangerous attempt to break through Allied lines in France. It came close to success, and had it not been halted, Germany might still have won the war. The French army had been bled white in 1917, and the smaller British Army was stretched to breaking point on a fifty-mile front. The British, supported by Australian, Canadian and New Zealand divisions and troops from many other countries, had in the first days thrown cooks and clerks and non-combatants into the front lines. Of the soldiers fighting on the Western Front, two hundred thousand were Irishmen, and of these fifty thousand had already laid down their lives. Most of them, like the prominent nationalist MPs Willie Redmond and Tom Kettle, had enlisted voluntarily. Against the epic drama being played out in Europe, the activities of men like Collins and de Valera seemed in British eyes to be insignificant, and Lloyd George allowed himself to be persuaded to extend conscription to Ireland.

The situation that spring was, after all, critical, but the depth of feeling against conscription in Ireland was fatally underestimated. In the event, its extension to Ireland was not strategically necessary. Germany had committed the last of its resources to the offensive and the United States, which had come into the war in 1917, was now pouring troops into the Front. In terms of manpower alone, Germany would soon have to sue for peace.

UFTM

Collins addressing an open air meeting

In February 1918 Collins had addressed a Sinn Féin meeting in Ballinamuck, County Longford, advising the young men of the area to join the Volunteers, to drill and to work in earnest to be ready for independence. It was now up to the Irish people to decide whether they would demand independence or remain 'a vassal state of John Bull' (Documents 35 and 36, pp. 91–4).

At the beginning of March Collins went to Longford again and stayed at the Greville Arms with the Kiernans. On 3 March, a cold Sunday, he addressed a meeting at Legga chapel after the second Mass. Beginning by saying that he did not know much about speech-making but that he 'knew a little about the working of the GPO in Easter week', he spoke about the hopeless failure of the Irish Convention which had just been wound up. It had been rigged by Lloyd George and did not represent the Irish people. Any solution it had reached would have been worse than 'that attempted at the partition scheme' (a reference to the failed attempts to find an Ulster solution in 1914). After casting some aspersions on the Orangemen and the Ulster Volunteers in Armagh, he returned to the political situation in the South, where 'the old set were at work again, trying to discredit our organisation'. However, the central message of his speech was that his audience should not take part in raids for arms from their neighbours, or in cattle drives. When the Volunteers raided for arms, he said, they should go 'where they will find [arms] that will be of some use to them' (Document 38, pp. 96–7).

Such a clear incitement to raid the police and military for weapons was the evidence the RIC was waiting for. The 'mental notes' of the police officers present were duly sent to the office of the county inspector in Longford and to the DMP in Dublin (Documents 38 and 39, pp. 96–8). A warrant was obtained for Collins's arrest, and sent to the DMP for execution (Document 45, p. 105). He returned to Dublin that evening, and a few days later he travelled to Limerick and then to Cork on the same organisational business.

He was arrested in Dublin on 2 April, as he left his office in Bachelor's Walk, by two of the DMP's men, O'Brien and Bruton. He resisted strenuously and a sympathetic crowd gathered, cheering him on, but he was taken across O'Connell Bridge to the Brunswick Street station. According to Collins's diary, quoted by Meda Ryan, he was kept for a few hours in 'a filthy, ill-ventilated cell', then taken to the Bridewell in a cab, accompanied by uniformed policemen and two detectives, Smith and Thornton. They asked him how things were in the south, to show that they knew about his recent movements. At six o'clock the next morning he was 'rudely awakened' and taken by train to Longford. Following Volunteer policy, he refused to recognise the court and was remanded in custody until the Longford Assizes, charged with having made a speech at Legga 'likely to cause disaffection'. It was not Volunteer policy to put up bail, so he was sent to Sligo jail. He was in a mood of black depression at the interruption to his work and he knew none of the other prisoners, so he occupied his time in reading Irish history.

When Helen Kiernan came to visit him on 10 April and bring him news of Granard, he persuaded her to stay in town overnight and visit him again next day. The same day he wrote to his sister Hannie in London. He was anxious to know 'what Lloyd George has done about conscription for this country. If he goes for it – well, he's ended.'

Lloyd George did go for it. The Military Service Bill was passed on 16 April. The Irish Parliamentary Party withdrew from the House of Commons in protest and never returned. Two days later the lord mayor of Dublin convened a meeting in the Mansion House to adopt two resolutions drawn up by de Valera. The first, a pledge to resist conscription, was to be signed at the door of every Catholic church on the following Sunday. The second simply declared that the passage of the Conscription Bill must be regarded as a declaration of war on the Irish nation.

On the same day the Catholic bishops, meeting at Maynooth, declared that the act was an oppressive and inhuman law 'which the Irish people have a right to resist by any means that are consonant with the law of God'. By sanctifying the resistance to conscription, and by implication the entire challenge to British rule in Ireland, the Church had in effect given its blessing to that challenge. The Catholic Church's shift of allegiance from the Irish Parliamentary Party to Sinn Féin was deeply significant, but it had been in prospect for some time. In part it simply reflected the changing mood of the people, but even before the end of the nineteenth century, the Catholic hierarchy had sensed that Ireland would soon be independent in one form or another, and it had a deep suspicion of anti-clerical influences in the Irish Parliamentary Party.

The electoral effects were apparent at once. Sinn Féin had not so far in 1918 been able to continue the successes of the previous year. Sean Milroy had been defeated two weeks earlier in East Tyrone, but now in the by-election pending in Offaly the Irish Parliamentary Party candidate actually withdrew, allowing the Sinn Féiner to be returned unopposed. Conscription had sounded the death knell of the Irish Parliamentary Party, which was virtually to disappear in the general election later in the year, and its withdrawal from the British parliament was a reluctant endorsement of the policy of abstention.

The country now seemed to be on the brink of rebellion and, according to Field Marshal Sir Henry Wilson (who was later to be assassinated by the IRA), Lloyd George impressed on the military authorities that the onus of shooting first must be placed on the Irish. The executive of the Volunteers decided to abandon the policy of refusing to recognise the courts or give bail. At this juncture men like Collins were more useful out of prison than in. Consequently Collins agreed to bail and left Sligo for Granard, where the streets were lined with supporters waiting to welcome him

'The country now seemed on the brink of rebellion': British troops searching for suspects

(Documents 47 and 48, pp. 107–9).

Collins slipped away from Sligo jail so quietly that the authorities in Dublin Castle seem to have been taken unawares (Document 47, p. 107). The original warrant for his arrest and the proceedings at Longford gave rise to a protracted legal paper-chase which went on until the late summer of the following year, by which time he was the most wanted man in Ireland. In June 1918 the Crown obtained an order in the High Court of Justice removing the case to the next assizes in the City of Londonderry (Documents 57 and 58, pp. 120-2). He failed to appear when his trial came up on 17 July, and the RIC had to confess that his whereabouts were unknown to them. The bail was forfeited and a bench warrant was issued for the arrest of the accused on sight (Documents 72 and 73, pp. 141–3).

With feeling in the country now running so high, this was a matter that required a political decision by the Government. The advice of the attorney general was sought, and the inspector general was duly informed that it was not proposed for the time being 'to arrest persons merely for internment' so the original warrant might be regarded as temporarily suspended. However, there was no discretion open to the Government with regard to the court warrant. 'And of course care will be taken to execute it in the manner least calculated to cause public disturbance or excitement . . .' (Document 67, p. 135). In the circumstances, the police were unclear about the course of action to take, and the DMP, who knew very well where to find Collins, were distinctly lacking in enthusiasm. Meanwhile back in Longford the Crown solicitor, T.W. Delany, told the county inspector that on the attorney general's instructions 'no further proceedings need be taken' (Document 81, p. 154). There was, however, yet another warrant outstanding, issued by the magistrates after Collins's speech at Skibbereen on 31 March 1918 (Document 84, p. 157).

The conscription crisis had a number of important consequences. Realising that tough measures would be required if the Act were to be enforced, Lloyd George made certain changes in the Irish administration. Lord Wimborne, the lord lieutenant, was replaced by Field Marshal Lord French, with new increased emergency powers, and an appropriate new title, Lord Lieutenant General and General Governor of Ireland. A new chief secretary was appointed, Edward Shortt, and changes made in the key posts in the Castle administration. The Government feared, from the activities of Collins and the other Sinn Féin leaders, that a new rebellion was being plotted. French, of senior military rank to the commander in chief of the forces in Ireland, soon made his presence felt. On the night of 17 May 1918 de Valera, Griffith, Count Plunkett, Darrell Figgis, Countess Markievicz, Joseph McGuinness, Sean McGarry and seventy other Sinn Féin activists, including Kathleen Clarke, were arrested and deported to English jails.

Collins had been warned of the impending arrests by one of his spies in the DMP, and went to alert McGarry, president of the IRB. Arriving at McGarry's house on his bicycle, he saw that the military raid was in progress, and he blended in among the curious crowd. He afterwards spent the night in McGarry's house, reckoning it to be the safest in Dublin. The official reason given for the arrests was that 'certain subjects of His Majesty the King, domiciled in Ireland, have conspired to enter into, and have entered into, treasonable communication with the German enemy'. There was no lack of will for such communication – de Valera was to say, 'Germany is not our enemy' – but the Government produced little evidence of a German plot. The Germans *had* sent one Joseph Dowling, an Irish prisoner of war, to Ireland by submarine in the hope of establishing contact with Sinn Féin, but he had been captured in April, on an island off the Galway coast. An ex-lance corporal of the Connaught Rangers, Dowling was one of the men Sir Roger Casement had recruited into his Irish Brigade.

The increasingly anti-British tone of the anti-conscription campaign was demonstrated at a meeting held in Skibbereen on 31 March 1918 in support of Bernie O'Driscoll, who was on hunger-strike in Cork jail

(Document 52, pp. 113–14). He had been imprisoned for saying at an earlier meeting in the same town that if Ernest Blythe, another hunger-striker, should die, then the Volunteers would know what to do. In court O'Driscoll had shouted, 'Up the Germans', and Collins, addressing the meeting, said that the Germans must have heard because that day they captured fifteen thousand British soldiers.

He repeated O'Driscoll's remark about reprisals, for the benefit of the police taking mental notes. Gearóid O'Sullivan went farther. The report-edly callous attitude of German U-boat commanders towards the crews of sinking British ships had provoked calls in Britain for retaliation against German prisoners-of-war. The Germans announced that, if this happened, they would shoot five British officers for every German prisoner ill-treated. Much of this was of course merely press comment in wartime, of dubious provenance, but it went down well with the audience, and O'Sullivan used it to threaten the police with reprisals if Sinn Féin pris-oners were punished. The speeches were duly reported by Constable McCarthy and Sergeant Malone (Documents 52 and 53, pp. 113–16).

Ernest Blythe was a maverick northern Protestant from Lisburn, County Antrim, frequently in prison for seditious speeches. A member of the IRB executive, he had embraced the cause with the zeal of the con-vert. In an article in *An t-Óglach*, the Volunteer journal, he went much farther than Collins, writing that anyone who assisted the implementation of conscription 'should be killed without mercy or hesitation as soon as opportunity offers'. Those who helped 'the enemy' should 'be shot, or otherwise destroyed, with the least possible delay'. Collins liked the article, and had hundreds of extra copies of it printed and distributed to the Volunteer brigades. It was a portent of what was to come.

So intense was public reaction that the Government backed off con-scription in the summer of 1918, and the end of the war in November removed it from the political agenda altogether. But by now the Volun-teers were stronger than ever. As director of organisation and (from March) adjutant general, Collins worked tirelessly on the structure of what would become the IRA. Ernie O'Malley, a young Volunteer officer, has left a vivid description of him at this time:

> He was pacing up and down. We shook hands. He jerked his
> head to a chair to indicate that I should sit; he took a chair
> which he tilted back against the wall. On the shelves were
> green membership cards, heaps of *The Irish Volunteer Hand-
> book*, and stacks of white copies of the organisation scheme.
> Behind his desk was a large map of Ireland marked with

broad red streaks radiating from Dublin. He was tall, his shoulders were broad; his energy showed through rapid movement. A curving bunch of hair fell on his forehead; he tossed it back with a vigorous head twist. 'I'm sending you to Offaly,' he said, 'I want you to organise a brigade in the county.'

Collins gave O'Malley a bundle of organisation schemes and instructions. He handed him notes on the destruction of railways, bridges and engines with and without explosives. He crossed to the window while O'Malley read them. 'My bail is up,' he said. 'They're looking for me now.' By 'they' he meant the G men.

Within a month of the ending of the war, Lloyd George called a general election. It was a bitter and bleak time of year; the newspapers were still filled with the names and faces of hundreds of servicemen killed in action, and a terrible influenza epidemic had begun to sweep through the population, claiming many lives. Sinn Féin decided to contest every seat in the country and the result was a landslide. Sinn Féin candidates won in seventy-three constituencies. The Unionists slightly strengthened their position by winning twenty-six seats. But the Irish Parliamentary Party was wiped out, and thereafter virtually ceased to exist, being reduced to six. Sinn Féin could now claim to represent the majority of people in Ireland.

1919

Collins, who had been one of the organisers of the Sinn Féin electoral campaign, was elected MP for South Cork, and in the New Year notices appeared in the newspapers that he would address a Sinn Féin meeting at his home town of Clonakilty on Sunday 5 January (Document 60, pp. 124–5). Collins's real reason for the visit was to reorganise the Cork Volunteers, and Dublin Castle ordered that he should be arrested if he appeared. The police applied to a magistrate for a warrant, pending the arrival of the bench warrant from Derry (Document 63, p. 127).

Meanwhile, the army took a hand. Since September 1918 the West Riding of Cork had been under virtual martial law, and the commandant of the military area now prohibited the meeting at Clonakilty. The police soon learned that the venue had been changed to Dunmanway, where

Collins addressing electors at Clonakilty, County Cork

Collins was determined to appear. The result was an attempt to arrest him by a joint RIC and army party. There was a police baton-charge, but Collins got away through the fields and escaped. Next day he was in Dublin helping to prepare for the opening of Dáil Éireann. The story of his escape is told in Document 66, pp. 131–4.

Following the principles laid down years before by Arthur Griffith, the

Sinn Féin members did not take their seats at Westminster, and on 21 January 1919 they met in Dublin as an Irish parliament, Dáil Éireann, in the Mansion House, the official residence of Dublin's lord mayor. Collins was not present on this occasion. A later, more formal meeting of the new Dáil was held on 1 April. The names of Unionist MPs such as Sir Edward Carson and Sir James Craig were solemnly read out, and marked *as láthair* ('absent'). De Valera was elected president of the new assembly, and next day he announced his cabinet. Collins was appointed minister of finance.

Soon after Dáil Éireann was set up, de Valera put forward the idea of a National Loan. 'It is obvious that the work of our Government cannot be carried out without funds. The Minister of Finance is accordingly preparing a prospectus which will shortly be published for the issue of a loan of one million pounds sterling – £500,000 to be offered to the public for immediate subscription . . . in bonds and such amounts as to meet the needs of the small subscriber.' De Valera and Collins disagreed on the wording of the prospectus (Document 89, pp. 164–6). Collins wanted some reference to the inspiration of the scheme, the Fenian Bonds issued in the 1860s, and even a promise that the Republic would honour them, but the pragmatic de Valera was resolutely opposed to this, and in his pedantic way irritated Collins by going through the document with him word by word.

The entire burden of responsibility for advertising the loan, collecting it

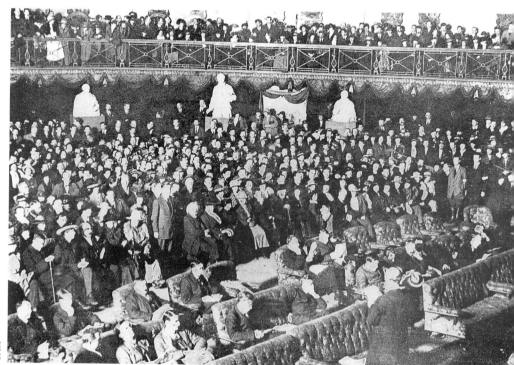

Dáil Éireann meeting in the Mansion House, Dublin, April 1919

and issuing the receipts fell on the young minister of finance, still in his twenties, and it is a measure of his efficiency that he carried it through successfully while holding at least four other posts and at the same time directing a campaign of guerrilla warfare.

Collins showed an uncanny prescience of the power of the cinema in propaganda. At a time when film was still something of a novelty, he had a short clip made in which he and Diarmuid O'Hegarty were shown sitting at a table outside Pearse's old school and signing bonds purchased by Pearse's mother, Clarke's widow and Connolly's daughter. It was used to good effect in the United States, from where Boland wrote to him: 'Gee, Boy. You are some movie actor. Nobody could resist buying a Bond and we having such a handsome Minister for Finance.' In Ireland the IRA over the next year went into cinemas, forced the projectionist at gunpoint to show the clip, and then disappeared before the police and military could arrive. The brief film brought Collins's name and image before the public as never before. All this was the more remarkable because Collins had taken great pains to prevent the police from having a reliable photograph of him. As late as 1921, during the Treaty negotiations in London, he instinctively moved his head each time a photograph was taken, so that the image was blurred.

Collins did not like the Loan work, and resented having to spend so much time on it. A year later he was complaining to Boland: 'The enterprise will certainly break my heart if anything ever will. I never imagined there would be so much cowardice, dishonesty, hedging, insincerity, and meanness in the world, as my experience of this work has revealed.' Nevertheless the National Loan ultimately raised £357,000, despite all the efforts of the authorities to prevent its collection. It was, of course, declared illegal at the outset, but only £18,000 of it was ever impounded by the authorities. The efforts to trace the funds led to one of the worst murders committed in 1920. On 26 March a retired civil servant and magistrate, Alan Bell, was dragged off a tramcar in Dublin city centre and shot dead. None of the other terrified passengers dared go to his assistance. The murder caused great revulsion in the British press and created bad publicity for Sinn Féin. What Collins knew was that Bell was a trusted personal friend of the viceroy, and was one of the three-man committee French had appointed to take a tougher line with terrorism, his particular task being to track down the National Loan deposits in various banks.

The Anglo-Irish War had begun on 21 January 1919, the day on which Dáil Éireann had its first meeting, when two RIC constables were shot dead at Soloheadbeg in County Tipperary. They were escorting a consignment of explosives being delivered to a mine. The

An RIC funeral, *c.* 1919

ambush had been organised and carried out by local Volunteers, led by Dan Breen and Seán Treacy, without the sanction of the Volunteer high command. Mulcahy, the chief of staff, at once condemned it as 'an ill-judged action with regrettable and unwarranted features'. Collins, though he approved of it, had no responsibility; he was in fact in England, organising the spectacular escape of 'German Plot' prisoners de Valera, McGarry and Milroy from Lincoln jail.

By June, following the shooting of a resident magistrate in Ballina and another three policemen, more areas were put under martial law. Collins had long been building up an intelligence network to rival that of the Castle, and this gave him a clear advantage in the initial stages of the war. After his nocturnal visit to DMP headquarters in Brunswick Street on 7 April, he had wasted no time in warning the Dublin detectives not to pursue him and his associates with undue zeal. On 9 April a party of Volunteers called on Detective Sergeant Halley at his home. On the same day Constable O'Brien was accosted in the street, gagged and left tied to the railings of the police station. Neither man was hurt, and O'Brien said later that it was 'damned decent' of Sinn Féin to have warned him.

Others were less lucky. Detective Sergeant Patrick Smith, while appreciating a friendly warning from neighbours, would not be deflected from his duty 'by the likes of Collins'. He had arrested Piaras Béaslaí, who would later be Collins's first biographer, for making a seditious speech. But he had also found incriminating documents on him, which would have meant a much more severe sentence. Collins and Boland tried to persuade Smith not to introduce the documents in court, but he ignored them. Collins was then authorised by Mulcahy to have Smith eliminated, and to form a special squad to assassinate detectives. Smith was shot and mortally wounded outside his home at Drumcondra on 30 July 1919.

The detectives of G Department of the DMP who became targets were generally those who proved dangerous to Collins, because they were getting too close to his operations. Detective Constable Daniel Hoey who had been involved in a raid on Sinn Féin headquarters at 6 Harcourt Street on 12 September, when Collins had almost been caught, was shot dead the same night. Detective Sergeant John Barton was gunned down in College Street during the rush hour on 30 November. Some of Collins's actions related to things done in 1916; Hoey had been the detective who had picked out Seán MacDermott among the prisoners at Richmond Barracks. In 1920 Collins discovered that Captain Lea-Wilson, a British officer who had ill-treated the 1916 prisoners, among them Tom Clarke, was a district inspector at Gorey in County Wexford. He had him shot at once.

Collins's squad of selected gunmen were to become known as the Twelve Apostles, though their numbers actually varied. They were paid four pounds and ten shillings a week, and they were able to strike with such deadly effect because Collins had infiltrated the DMP, the RIC and the Castle. Four of the G men were his agents. Detective Sergeant Joseph Kavanagh recruited James MacNamara, Ned Broy and David Neligan. MacNamara was a confidential clerk in the Castle, and was trusted because he was the son of a policeman and also from a Unionist background. Broy, as we have seen, was a confidential typist at Brunswick Street, and made an extra copy for Collins of every secret report he typed. In 1933 he was appointed commissioner of the Garda Síochána. Neligan, the youngest of the four, had joined the DMP in 1918. After some months as a G man he had offered to work for the British secret service and been accepted. He remained undetected until the British withdrawal in 1922. He published his memoirs, *The Spy in the Castle*, in 1968, at which time it was claimed that he was drawing five pensions – from the IRA, the RIC, the Garda Síochána, the Irish civil service and the British Secret Service!

Collins could rely also on the help of a small band of devoted women agents who worked as clerks and typists in the GPO or the Castle. They included his cousin, Nancy O'Brien, who became John Collins's second wife in 1922. It is even said that in 1918 Sir James MacMahon, later to be joint under-secretary at the Castle, entrusted her with all the Castle's secret coded messages. Collins's incredulous response was to wonder how the British ever acquired an Empire.

Scene of the assassination attempt on Lord French, December 1919

1 9 2 0

After an unsuccessful attempt to assassinate the lord lieutenant on 19 December 1919, the intended victim complained that 'our secret service is simply non-existent . . . the DMP are absolutely demoralised and the RIC will be in the same case very soon if we do not quickly set our house in order'. As part of the effort to carry out this directive, Detective Inspector W.C. Forbes Redmond was brought from Belfast and appointed assistant commissioner of police to reorganise the G Division. He brought with him some of his own detectives and people prepared to work under cover. Not knowing Dublin well, he turned to his administrative assistant, James MacNamara, for advice, and outlined to him his plans for capturing Collins. Redmond did not have a high opinion of the Dublin detectives. 'You were supposed to be looking for Collins,' he told them. 'You have been after him for months and never caught sight of him, while a new man, just over from England, met him and talked to him after two days.'

With these fatal words Redmond sent to his death an English agent, and sealed his own fate, because MacNamara relayed the remarks to Collins, who was soon able to identify the spy. Calling himself Jameson, he had posed as an English communist agitator, who fraternised with Irish conspirators in London and had come to Dublin, met IRB leaders, and offered to help with gun running. He returned to England, while Redmond used his information to carry out a raid which came within a millimetre of success. Once again, as so often, Collins had the luck not to be recognised. Three days later, Redmond was shot dead outside the Standard Hotel in Harcourt Street. Jameson, whose real name was apparently Burns, and who was the son of a police officer from Limerick, was later described as 'one of the best and cleverest Secret Service men that England ever had'. He went back to Ireland twice more, but on 2 March two of the Apostles called for him at his hotel in Sackville Street and, on the pretext of taking him to Collins, conveyed him to a lonely playing-field and shot him through the head and heart.

After Redmond's murder the authorities offered a reward of £10,000 for information about the perpetrators. It was never claimed. His undercover detectives returned to Belfast, and the G Division effectively ceased to operate against Collins and his organisation. By now, too, the RIC was crumbling, with an increasing number of officers defecting to Collins's side. His greatest strength was the tacit support of a large proportion of the civil population. When he tried to extend his operations to the North, however, the consequences were different. There the actions of the IRA

A combined army and RIC patrol

only served to ignite the age-old sectarian war, and though it was, if anything, even more bloody, its outcome was less predictable.

The file on Collins ends at the point where the British government began to intensify its operations against the IRA. Among the last documents are some reports on Collins annotated by Redmond just a day or two before his death (Document 95, p. 174; Document 97, p. 176; Document 99, p. 178). On 24 February a curfew was imposed on Dublin from midnight until 5.00 a.m. It was the collapse of the police system which led to the recruitment and use of the Black and Tans and the Auxiliaries, and the ascending spiral of atrocity and reprisal which made 1920 and 1921 years of terror in Ireland. The story of that war has been told and retold elsewhere, of how it led to the Treaty negotiations and the establishment in twenty-six counties of Ireland of the Irish Free State, now the Republic of Ireland.

Collins campaigning at Naas, County Kildare, in support of the treaty

UFTM

In the early hours of 6 December 1921, five years after his Christmas release from Frongoch, Michael Collins signed his name in Irish to the Articles of Agreement for a Treaty, and at once admitted that he had probably signed his own death warrant. During the 'troubles' Lloyd George had tried to solve one part of the Irish Question by passing the fourth Government of Ireland Act of 1920. It set up two parliaments, one in Dublin and one in Belfast. The southern parliament was stillborn, but the northern parliament, first at Belfast City Hall and then at Stormont, continued to govern Northern Ireland as part of the United Kingdom until it was suspended in 1972. In the South, however, the bitter debates in the Dáil over the acceptance of the Treaty led finally to a brief and vicious civil war. It was not the civil war which for so long had seemed to be impending, between Catholic and Protestant, North and South. Instead it was a war between Catholic and Catholic, between Free Stater and Republican, though the future of the North and the question of partition were largely the reasons for it.

Collins at Griffith's funeral in August 1922, where he acted as a pallbearer. His own funeral was to follow only twelve days later.

The motives which impelled General Michael Collins, in August 1922, to include his native county in his tour of inspection of places held by the National Army are still debated by historians. The area was solidly republican, and occupied by the anti-treaty IRA, the Irregulars, most of whom were his former comrades in arms. At 6.00 a.m. on the morning of 22 August he left the city of Cork, hoping to get as far west as Bantry. The convoy consisted of an open Crossley tender equipped with a Lewis gun, a Leyland Thomas touring car and an armoured car, also with machine-guns. The first stop was Macroom then on to Bandon. From Bandon they made for Clonakilty where the whole town turned out to meet him. At Woodfield his brother John came in from the fields, and he had a drink with his family and neighbours.

They pressed on to Skibbereen, where they decided to return to Cork. Five miles along the twisting road beyond Bandon, at a desolate spot called Béal na mBláth, the convoy was ambushed by Irregulars. A hail of machine-gun fire swept the road and shattered the windscreen of the car. They could have sped away, but Collins ordered his men to stand and fight, and there was an exchange of fire for about half an hour. The light was fading and, as the attackers began to draw off, one took a last shot at the officer he saw standing in the road.

The bullet struck Collins behind his left ear and he died a few seconds later.

Collins's funeral cortège leaving Dublin's pro-cathedral, 28 August 1922

THE
DOCUMENTS

181 5
75522

(1858.) Wt.5333—66.4000.12/14. A.T.&Co.,Ltd.
(6559.) Wt.3103—96.20,000.8/15.

Telegrams: "DAMP, DUBLIN."
Telephone No. 22.

DUBLIN METROPOLITAN POLICE.

Detective Department,

SECRET.

Dublin, 8th January,   191 7.

Subject, _____ MICHAEL COLLINS, SUNDAY'S WELL, CORK, - RELEASED PRISONER.

With reference to the attached, I beg to report that
Michael Collins, clerk, native of Cork, who was a member of
the Irish Volunteers, lodged at 16, Rathdown Road, Dublin.
He left his lodgings on Easter Monday and did not return there
afterwards. He was in the general surrender of the rebels
at Richmond Barracks on Sunday, 30th April, 1916 and was
deported to England and interned there. He did not return to
his lodgings since his release.

Geo. Love.

Inspector.

The Supt., G Division.

The Chief Commr
Submitted
Owen Brien
Supt
8. 1. '7

The Inspector General R.I.C.
Transmitted.
Col. Johnstone
Comm 8/1/17.

C/. Clerk
For further report please regarding
his men.
J S Robinson

9/1/17   Cl. for reg

Michl. Collins released
Sinn Fein (interned) prisoner
Circular 27.12.16

Crime Special

S.
4438
D.M.P.

218
76008

County of Cork W.R.

Clanakilty 31.12.16

I beg to report that
on 16th inst Michael
Collins a native of
Woodfield Miltown
Sub Dist. returned to
his brothers home in
this District. He was
not arrested in this
District or at the instance
of the Dist police in
any way. This young man
was employed in the Post
office — in Dublin I understand
latterly — and was
apprehended for some
connection recent rebellion
or Sinn Feinism there,
He boasts to his friends
that he was in the rebellion
fighting in Church
street Dublin for four
days
the County Inspector
Bandon

C.I. D.M.P.

Transmitted for information &
for favour of report as to his
history in Dublin.
He is apparently not the Mr. Collins
Clerk of Dublin — who is now at
Sunday's Well Cork. (Your $\frac{5}{4378}$ 8/1/17)

J E Woodhens

C.I. for D.I.G.
9.1.17

Supt. G div
wr J

10.1.17

He is a young man of
fair complexion clean
shaven strong jaws
and features may
be 28 years of age,
He belongs to a family
"brainy" people who
are disloyal and
of advanced Sinn
Fein sympathies
They are of the farming
class

J.M.Lowden
W

Bandon 6·1·17
Submitted·

T. Tweedy
CI.

The Insp. General

2941

Release of interned prisoners.

Crime—Special.

Hd.-Qrs. File No. 181 S.
75522

COUNTY OF Cork City

Cork 8.1.17.

Referring to file

181 S 26.12.16. I beg
75522

to report that Collins has not so far come to Cork.

This man is a native of Cork, but he has not resided here for years past. He was employed in Dublin prior to the rebellion and was arrested and interned from there. His address in Dublin was 16 Rath-down Road.

Collins has a sister residing at Sunday's Well. Cork. She is married to a man The C.I. named

C.C. one.

Perhaps this man is the Michael Collins — now in Cork W.R. referred to in file 248 S 76008 sent you on 9th inst.

J.S. Holmes

Ct. Insp
13/1/17

Supt. Lynn

Dunn
Asst Comm 5/

name a Powell, an
Exeise Officer serving
in Cork.

There is nothing
know of Collins here.

A.Young.
Sgt 48585.

Cork 8.1.17.
Submitted.

C.d.Walsh

The J.G.   1 D1 for C.I.
on leave

218 S
76008

(1858.) Wt.5333—66.4000.12/14.A.T.&Co.,Ltd.
(6559.) Wt.5105—96.20,000.8/15.

Telegrams: "DAMP, DUBLIN."
Telephone No. 22.

DUBLIN METROPOLITAN POLICE.

Detective Department,

Dublin,_____ 17th January, **191**7.

R.I. CONSTABULARY OFFICE
Received
18 JAN 1917

SECRET.

Subject,_____ MICHAEL COLLINS - INTERNED PRISONER - RELEASED.

With reference to Files 4378/S and 4438/S, I beg to report that there is very little doubt that Michael Collins, Woodfield, Milltown, Co. Cork and the Michael Collins whose sister resides at Sunday's Well are one and the same person. Anyhow, I can trace only one man of the name interned from Dublin.

The man who lodged at 16, Rathdown Road was employed in the months of March and April, 1916, as temporary clerk in Messrs. Craig, Gardner & Co's, and is said to have been previously employed in the Post Office, London.

Geo. Love
Inspector.

The Supt.,
    G Division.

The Chief Commr
Submitted.
Owen Brien
Supt
17 . 1 . 17

The Inspector General R.I.C.
Transmitted.

C Comm 17/1/17

CI Cork
For Information. Return Through CI
Bandon.

18/1/17

Clonakilty 25 Jan'y 1917

Submitted, there is no
doubt Superintendent
Lane's report on this
matter is in accordance
with the facts. The Collins
family to which this
man Michl Collins belongs
is a very disloyal
and (if they could) a
dangerous family. John
Collins with whom Michael
has resided since his
liberation is an ardent
Sinn Feiner and even his
wife had a brother in
the Dublin rising who died
in hospital of his wounds
rec'd in the rebellion fighting.
Every member of the Collins
family is aggressively disloyal
and it is a dangerous thing to have
an Excise official connected
with them

Jno Lawlor RO

The County Insp. Bandon

Report Suspect Michael
Collins

Crime 8R

County of Cork. W.R.

Milltown 20: 5: 17.

I beg to state that Michael
Collins who was interned
for participation in Sinn
Fein Rebellion in Dublin
in 1916. came to reside with
his Brother. John M. Collins
of Woodfield this Sub District
shortly before Xmas last.
and remained there until
about about the end of January
when he went to Cork and
resided with his Sister Mrs
Powell at Sundays Well.

Collins I am informed
attended a large and
representative meeting of
Sinn Feiners in Cork which
was held I believe in February
last, and soon after went
to Dublin and was appointed
paid Secretary to the Sinn
Fein. organisation there.

This man during his
stay in this Sub District

The District Inspector

lived what may be
considered a retired life,
and no notice was taken
of his presence in the locality
by anyone.

I have made discreet
inquiry and I have failed
to find out who the Cheany
referred to in attached file
is, but I am satisfied
that Collins did not reside
there, but with his Sister
Mrs Powell at Sundayswell
he has not been in the
habit of visiting this
locality and I am not
aware of his ever having
visited it before

There is no doubt what-
ever that the Michael Collins
who was interned from Dublin
is the man who resided
with his Brother John A.
Collins of Woodfield is one
and the same person.

John Smith
Sgt 53443.

Clonakilty 22. 5. 17
Submitted.

The C.O. Insp.
Bandon

R.I. CONSTABULARY OFFICE
Received
29 MAY. 1917
Dublin Castle
CRIME SPECIAL BRANCH

R.I. CONSTABULARY OFFICE
Received
24 MAY. 1917
Dublin Castle
CRIME SPECIAL BRANCH

314
78090

Suspect Michael Collins

S.5039

Secret

County of Cork. W.R.

County Inspector's Office.
Bandon. 23rd May 1917

C1

Submitted.

T. Tweedy
CI

The Insp'd General.

I.

CC. DMP.

Transmitted.
Please see Clonakilty reports, by
which it would appear that he
is Secretary to the Sinn Fein Organization
He is evidently the man mentioned
on attached files.

L.G. Edwards

CI. Sp'l g
24/5/17

II.

Asst. G. divn.

bam 25/5
Sey

IV.

The Inspector General,

Transmitted.

W. Johnstone
CC 29/5/17

Detective Office
Dublin,
29. 5. 17

III.

I beg to state that Suspect
Michael Collins referred
to in this file is Secretary
of the Irish National Aid
and Volunteer Dependents'
Fund Association, 10
Exchequer Street.
The Supt. G.Dwr.   Geo Love.
                              Inspt

The Chief Comm
Submitted
Owen Brien 29/5

(1858.) Wt.5333—66.4000.12/14.A.T.&Co.,Ltd.
(6559.) Wt.3103—96.20,000.8/15.

Telegrams: "DAMP, DUBLIN."
Telephone No. 22.

S.
5039
D.M.P.

DUBLIN METROPOLITAN POLICE.

Detective Department,

Dublin, 16th April, 1917.

Subject, WAR "B" LIST SUSPECT JOHN MILROY TO LONGFORD.

I beg to report that Suspect John Milroy left

Broadstone to Longford by 5-10 p.m. train on 14th

inst.

His departure was notified by cipher telegram to the

District Inspector, R.I.C. there.

Geo. Love.
Inspector.

The Supt., G Division.

The Chief Commr
Submitted.
Owen Brien
Supt
16/4/17

The Inspector General,
Transmitted.

C Commr. 16/4

CI. Longford.
For report please.

Received 6·50 pm. on 14:4:'17

A

Prefix_____Code_____

POST OFFICE TELEGRAPHS.
(Inland Official Telegrams only.)

No. of Telegram_____

Office of Origin and Service Instructions.

Words.	Sent

O. H. M. S.

At_____.M.
To_____
By_____

I certify that this Telegram is sent on the service of the

(*Signature*)_____

Attention is called to the Regulations printed at the back hereof.

Dated Stamp.

TO{ District Inspector Longford.

By	Five	P M	train	to
Longford	John	Milroy	Number	eleven
War	B	List.		

FROM{ Damp Dublin

The **Name** and **Address** of the Sender, IF NOT TO BE TELEGRAPHED, should be written in the Space provided at the Back of the Form.

(5692) Wt. 8475-1248. 400,000. 6/10. Wy. & S., Ltd. **Sch.** 27

Sent at 9·40 am on 16:4:'17

A

Prefix_____Code_____

POST OFFICE TELEGRAPHS.
(Inland Official Telegrams only.)

No. of Telegram_____

Office of Origin and Service Instructions.

Words.	Sent

O. H. M. S.

At_____.M.
To_____
By_____

I certify that this Telegram is sent on the service of the

(*Signature*)_____

Attention is called to the Regulations printed at the back hereof.

Dated Stamp.

TO{ Damp Dublin

To	you	by	two	am
train	today	Suspect	John	Milroy

FROM{ Sergeant Reidy Longford.

The **Name** and **Address** of the Sender, IF NOT TO BE TELEGRAPHED, should be written in the Space provided at the Back of the Form.

(5692) Wt. 8475-1248. 400,000. 6/10. Wy. & S., Ltd. **Sch.** 27

Crime Special

Suspect John Milroy No. 11

D. U. P. War B. List.

~~Visit to Wexford 14-16 Apl 17~~

County of Longford

Longford 16th April 1917

I beg to report that the above
named arrived in this town
by train from Dublin at 7.50
Pm on 14th inst. He left for
Dublin by the 2 oc "night
mail" train for Dublin this
morning. Lawrence Ginnell
and Michael Collins 44 mountjoy St Dublin also arrived
with Milroy. They were met at
the station by all the leading
local Sinn Feiners, and two
Sinn Fein flags were carried.
Milroy put up at the "Longford
Arms Hotel" for the night;
and, accompanied by other
Sinn Feiners motored to several
outlying districts in south
Longford, where meetings were
(in yesterday)
held on behalf of the Sinn
Fein
The District Inspector

CC. DMP.
Transmitted —
Please ~ A

A
44 mount

Fein Candidate, and this was
his object in coming to Longford.
I attach Copies of deciphered
wires received and sent in
Connection with this man.

        Thomas Reidy Sergt. 56485

      Longford. 16. 4. 17.

      Submitted.

        E.S. Pristin 151

The C.I. Insp.

       County Inspector's Office
        Longford 16. 4. 17.

Submitted: these men are
engaged yesterday in
Canvassing for Joseph McGuinness
and attended meetings held
in the County

      Reynell Heard
          C.I.

The Insp. Genl.

(1858.) Wt.5333—66.4000.12/14. A.T.&Co.,Ltd.
(6559.) Wt.3103—96.20,000.8/15.

Telegrams: " DAMP, DUBLIN."
Telephone No. 22.

314
78099

DUBLIN METROPOLITAN POLICE.

Detective Department,

Dublin, ___4th May,___ 1917.

SECRET

Subject, ___ SUSPECT JOHN MILROY.

R.I. CONSTABULARY OFFICE
Received
6 — MAY 1917
Dublin Castle
SPECIAL BRANCH

With reference to "A" in this File, I beg to report
that Mr. Laurence Ginnell, M.P., was a passenger by the
same train as John Milroy on 14th ultimo from Broadstone
Station.

Michael Collins, Clerk, is living at 44, Mountjoy
Street since the end of January last. His previous address is believed to have been 3, Gardiner's Hill, Cork.

This may be the Michael Collins, native of Woodfield,
Clonakilty, who lodged at 16, Rathdown Road here before
the Rebellion, and who, on his release from Frongoch
before Christmas last year, took his discharge to Sunday's
Well, Cork, where his sister resides. P.P. Files S 4378
and S 4438.

Geo. Love

Inspector.

The Superintendent,

   G Division.

The Inspector General,

      Transmitted.

A. Cork.
For report please .
File re Mr Collins attached

The Chief Comms
Submitted.
Owen Breen
Supdt 4/5/17

Wm. Edmuntone
CC 4/6/17

7/5/19   CI for 19

Suspect John Milroy
and Michael Collins.

Crime—Special.

Hd.-Qrs. File No. 314 S.
78099.

COUNTY OF Cork City

Cork 14. 5. 17.

I beg to report that
number 3. Gardiner's
Hill. Cork. is occupied
by a family named
O'Leary. and no person
named Collins has
ever been known to
lodge there, nor in any
other house in that
locality.

Michael Collins,
native of Woodfield.
Clonakilty. has never
been known to lodge
in any place in Cork
except in his sister's
house at Sunday's Well.
and I have no idea
as to why his address
previous to January
                      last
The C.I.

D. Clonakilty.

For report please.

J.S. Holmes
                    U. Ireg
15/5/17

last should be given
as 3, Gardiner's Hill.
However two members
of the O'Leary family
are connected with the
Sinn Fein movement
here and it is possible
that one of them may
be communicating with
Collins.

. A. Young.
        Sgt 48585.

  Cork 14. 5. 17.
  Submitted.

                2. actrour
The IG   C. I.

3/4
80840

Crime Special

~Secret~
~Immediate~

COUNTY OF Longford

County Inspector's Office,

Longford 27 July 1917

Thomas Ashe accompanied by Arthur Griffith
left here by motor car LI 526. apparently
for Mullingar at 8.30 pm on 22nd inst
after the Sinn Fein demonstration here
The police at Mullingar did not pick him
up there. I reported to the I.G. on 26th inst that
they may have gone to Dublin —
When did Ashe arrive in Granard. Was
Arthur Griffith with him — He should be
closely watched, and his destination ascertained
A report should be made of his movements
while in your district.

Reginald _____

C.I.

C.I. Sligo
For report please.
J.G. _____
30/7/17   C.I. Sligo

S.I. Granard

GRANARD 28th July 1917.

I beg to state that Thomas Ashe
arrived here on 21st inst. by train,
accompanied by a young man named
Collins - also a discharged rebel. They
left for the meeting at Longford on
22nd either by motor car or on a
wagonette, and returned to Granard

THE COUNTY INSPECTOR.

On same evening. Griffiths was
not seen here. neither was motor car
I 1 526.
Ashe and Collins left here by train
on 27th Inst. and it is believed they
have gone to Keash Co. Sligo.
A report about Ashe's movements
was submitted yesterday.

Chas. Collins.
28.7.

COUNTY OF Longford.

County Inspector's Office,
Longford 29 July 1917

Submitted: Ashe has been in Granard Dist
organising Sinn Fein Clubs, as he was present
at one which was formed & was trying to start
others. He moved about while at Granard
with Paul D. Cusack & John Cawley. He
has now gone on 27th inst to Keash Co Sligo
A Sinn Feiner named Michael Collins who is alleged
to have been in the G P.O Dublin and fought there
during the rebellion was also with him. The Sergt at
Granard wrote by first post to Sergt at Keash informing
him.

The Insp Genl

Reginald Heard
C.I

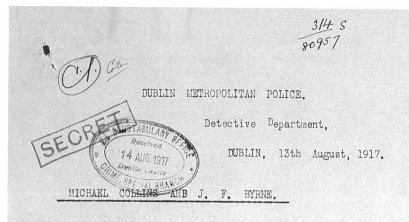

314 S
80957

DUBLIN METROPOLITAN POLICE.

Detective Department,

DUBLIN, 13th August, 1917.

SECRET

ROYAL IRISH CONSTABULARY OFFICE
Received
14 AUG 1917
Dublin Castle
CRIME SPECIAL BRANCH

MICHAEL COLLINS AND J. F. BYRNE.

The Inspector General,

Transmitted.

With reference to attached, I beg to state that Michael Collins was appointed paid Secretary to Irish National Aid in January, 1917 and in June last he became a member of the Executive Council of Sinn Fein.

His description is 28 years, 5ft. 10 ins. high, well built, square shoulders, dark brown hair, round face, clean shaven, pale complexion, wears grey tweed suit and brown trilby hat.

John F. Byrne is not known to the Special Staff here, nor can he, so far, be traced from inquiry.

V. Quinn
13/8/17   *ac*

F. Murphy
Chief Inspector.

The Supt.,
G Division.

A. Armagh
For information
Have you learnt any more
about JF Byrne – I have
give his description

J S Holmes

C.I. July 9
14/8/17

The Chief Comm
Submitted.
Owen Brien
Supt. 13/8/17

Armagh 14. 8. 17
For report
C. C. outlón
Sn. McFettigan

$\frac{314}{80957}$ S.5733

Michael Collins and
John J. Byrne.

Secret and Crime Special

County Armagh.

Armagh 16th. August. 1917.

I beg to state with reference to attached file
that John Joseph Byrne is the name. I am of opinion
that it was John J. Byrne I gave in my report
of 1st inst: as that is the name entered in the Register.

I attach a cutting from "The Catholic Bulletin" for
August 17 in which Byrnes' name figures under
the heading of "Events of Easter Week"

His description is:— Goodlooking active man,
pale complexion, regular face, medium make,
boyish looking, 5 ft 8 or 9 inches high and about 30
years of age, dark hair, clean shaven, wore a dark
suit and soft hat.

My informant is of opinion that he is attending
school yet.

Philip Mc Gettigan, S.55531.

C.C. D.I.P.
Please see description
press cutting re Byrne

18/8/17

The C.I.

Armagh 17th August '17
Submitted
C.C. Dublin

The I.G.

THE CATHOLIC BULLETIN

AND BOOK REVIEW

Vol. VII	AUGUST 1917	No. 8

EVENTS OF EASTER WEEK 513

JOHN JOSEPH BYRNE, q. 173, was born at Portarlington, but has resided in Dublin for many years. Member of the Colum Cille Branch of the Gaelic League and of the Irish Volunteers, he held a position at Kingsbridge in the same office as Com. Heuston, for serving under whom during Easter week he was sentenced to death.

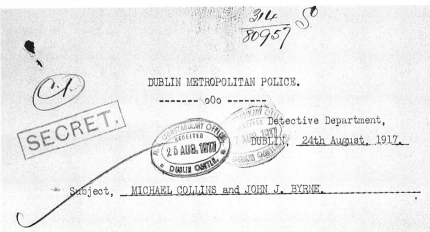

DUBLIN METROPOLITAN POLICE.

-------- oOo --------

Detective Department,

DUBLIN, 24th August, 1917.

Subject, __MICHAEL COLLINS and JOHN J. BYRNE.__

The Inspector General,

        Transmitted.

           a.c.

C.I. Armagh

For information

C.I. for I.G.
25:8:17.

> With further reference to attached,
> I beg to state that John J. Byrne resides
> at 24, Manor Place, Dublin, and was formerly
> employed as messenger in the Audit Dept. of
> the G. S. & W. Railway, Kingsbridge. He
> was a member of the Irish Volunteers, and
> took part in the Rising of Easter Week, '16.
> He was amongst those who surrendered to the
> military in the Mendicity Institution,
> Usher's Quay, on the collapse of the Re-
> bellion, and was sentenced to three years
> penal servitude by Courtmartial on 6th May,
> 1916.
>
> Beyond his being a member of the Irish
> Volunteers he was not otherwise prominent
> as a suspect.

                           P. Murphy

                           Chief Inspector.

The Supt.,

      G Division.

                   The Chief Commr

                   Submitted.

                   Owen Brien

                   Supt. 24/8/17

314
81999   S   101 / 185   Secret. Crime. Spcl.

No.   Michael Collins Sinn Fein Organiser,

County of Leitrim,
Carrick on Shannon 21: 8: 17,

    I beg to report that the above.
named arrived here from Dublin by
8.37 P.m. train on 18th. inst. He was
met on his arrival by the following.
person's. Denis Cassidy, Samuel E.
Holt, Thomas Candon, Francis Mc.Greevey
D. O.Driscol, all of Carrick on Shannon none of those are of any
importance, Collins went to the Bush.
Hotel where he remained for the night,
And on following day he left here at
11 am for to Gowel Leitrim Sub. Dist
where there is a Sinn Fein club.
returning to Carrick on Shannon same evening and aaddressed a meeting from 9 P.m.
to 9.45 P.m. for the purpose of forming a
Sinn Fein club. the speech was very.
moderate, At 10 P.m. he drove by car to
Drumlion, Co. Roscommon to form a
Sinn Fein club. And returned to Carrick-
on Shannon at 11.30 P.m. leaving by night
mail train for Dublin,

       Patrick, Bevine,
        Const 60, 298,
        Selected,

The. Dist Inspector,
    Carrick on Shannon
      22-8-17

Submitted
The C/I

W⁄184

Secret & C. Special

Gowel Sinn Fein Club.

Leitrim p. 19 - 8 - 17.

I beg to report that I attended at Gowel on this date as directed At 11½ am a man whom I afterward learned was of the name of Collins accompanied by a Shop boy of John Costelloes Carrick-on-Shannon. Named Casey. arrived at Gowel per Car They were met there by Thomas Duignan Sec. to the Gowel Sinn Fein Club. After mass Collins, Casey, The President Sec. & Treasurer of the Gowel club entered the Hall They were followed by about 140 young men, All remained in the hall from 1¼ to 1.35 pm. I am informed Collins addressed them on the principles and aims of the Sinn Fein movement. The total membership of this club is now 30. members, and it is expected all the young men in S.D. will become members. The meeting was not advertised.

J Thornton Sgt 33722

The D.I.

Of Carrick-on-Shannon.
Who is this man Collins and
where did he come from?

C, for I.G.
23/8/17

A

Carrick-on-Shannon. 20-8-17
'A' is too vague, what did Collins actually say
WHHassey DI

The Sergt Leitrim

Leitrim p. 21. 8. 17.

I beg to state as this meeting was held in doors. The fact of it being 4½ miles from this Stn. & those attending same are all Young men most of whome are residents of Drumsna, & Keshcarrigan Sub Dists. I am unable to give the exact words used by Collins. I regret not being able to supply my Officer with more information regarding this meeting, but under the circumstances named I am unable.

J. Thornton

Sergt P.C. Sq 53722.

Carrick-on-Shannon

22-8-17

Submitted   As far as can be ascertained that object of meeting was to increase membership of local Sinn Fein club.

At the present, it is almost impossible to ascertain definitely what transpires at indoor Sinn Fein meetings. It can be readily understood that "anti Conscription" and "formation of a Republic for Ireland" are the usual & sole subjects discussed at these meetings.

W. H. Juss Sgt. P.C.

The C.I.

Carrick on Shannon 22. 8. 17

Submitted.

The Inspr. General.

Ross C Rainsford
Co. Inspr

314/83142 S° Crime Special

9P's
Att^d

Suspect Michl Collins
Released rebel prisoner

Cl. County of Cork

Clonakilty 26 . 9 .

[stamp: R.I. CONSTABULARY — 26 SEP 1917 — CRIME S.]

I beg to report the above named
suspect has recently been visiting
the Bantry and Skibbereen Districts
organising Sinn Fein clubs and
making speeches to Sinn Feiners.
This young man is a native
of Woodfield Sub Dist of Rosscarbery
is the son of a farmer and belongs
to a family of dangerous extremists
He resided in Dublin before the
Rebellion of last year and took
part in the fighting that occurred
there. He sometimes resides (or
did reside before going to Dublin)
in Cork City where his sister
is married to an Excise officer
named Powell He is I am satisfied
well known to the Cork City
police and is also well known
to the D. M. P. after his

29/9

The Co Inspr Bandon

K
5401

release from internment after
the rebellion he came back to his
native place for a short time
and returned to Dublin where
he was appointed Secretary or
assistant Secretary to the Sinn
Fein association. Please see
file $\frac{314}{78099}$ S 15:5:17 respecting
this man and his movements
also $\frac{218}{76008}$ S 18:1:17. Atta to 78099 He came
back to his native place on
11th ulto and attended the
Skibbereen Sinn Fein demonstration
on the following day. He returned
to Cork on 12th ulto. He is no
doubt since in Dublin at his
post as paid Secretary of the ⎫ "A"
Sinn Fein Head Quarters. He took ⎬
part in the Clare election on
the Sinn Fein side and is likely
to become a prominent and
important member of that body
Callins is about 5'9 inches high 3 years of age
stout build sallow complexion [signature]
dark hair

Bandon 25th September 1917
Submitted for information.
Please see "A".
The Inspr General   " Genl 1st for C.
on Inspn

218 S
3,102

Secret

Crime Special

Sinn Fein Executives ..

Co. Cork W.R.
Bandon 24:12:17

With reference to C.S. Circular of 5th
instant on above subject, I beg
to report that there are 4 Parliamentary
Divisions in this Riding as follows:-
South East Cork, West Cork,
South Cork, & Mid Cork.
As regards the Parliamentary Division
of South East Cork which extends
into Cork E.R., (1) No Sinn Fein
Executive has yet been selected.
(2) No person has yet been selected
to represent the Division on the
governing body of Sinn Fein.
(3) No person has yet been selected
as the Sinn Fein Candidate for
a Parliamentary vacancy.

In the Parliamentary Division
of West Cork (1) No Sinn Fein Executive
has yet been selected so far as the
Police are aware.
(2) Daniel Sweeney, Ardnagehy,
Bantry, a farmer's son & civil Engineer,
was selected (at a meeting held
in Bantry on 18th Nov 17) to represent
the Division on the governing body
The Inspector General

of Sinn Fein, & attended the Sinn Fein Convention in Dublin. He was accompanied by Ernest Blythe who is in Bantry as Gaelic League organizer & who was at the Convention elected on the Sinn Fein Executive Council.

(3) No person has yet been selected as the Sinn Fein candidate for a Parliamentary vacancy in the Division of West Cork.

For the South Cork Parliamentary Division an Executive has been formed at Rosscarbery known as the "South Cork Sinn Fein Executive."

(1) Joseph M Cullinane, Solicitor, Clonakilty, has been appointed President. Peter O'Hourihane, Poundlick Skibbereen, has been appointed Vice President, Frederick Calanan, Rosscarbery & Michael Ahern, Clonakilty, are Treasurers & Joseph Flynn, Clonakilty, Secretary. The following are members of the Committee:- John Collins, Woodfield, Clonakilty; James Cahalane, Clonakilty, & John Donovan, Ardagh, Rosscarbery.

(2) Joseph M Cullinane, Solicitor, Clonakilty has been selected to represent the Division on the governing body of Sinn Fein. He is a Solicitor of poor practice & is about 30 years of age.

Until recently he never took part in
politics but for the past 6 months he
has developed into an advanced
Sinn Feiner.

(3) Michael Collins, late of Woodfield
Clonakilty, + who took part in the
fighting during the Rebellion
in Dublin in Easter week, has been
selected as the Sinn Fein candidate
for a Parliamentary vacancy in
the Division, should it arise.
He was interned after the Rebellion
+ was released at the general
amnesty of prisoners last year.
He is now residing in Dublin &
holds the post of paid Secretary to
the Sinn Fein movement there.

       For the Parliamentary Division
of Mid Cork a Sinn Fein meeting was
held at Macroom 25/10/17 + an
Executive elected for Mid Cork
known as the "Mid Cork Sinn Fein
Executive".
       The following is its composition:-

(1) President - Denis Lynch, Draper,
              New Street, Macroom.
Vice President - Daniel Corkery, Grocer,
              Cork Street, Macroom.
Secretary - Denis Creedon Drapers-
              clerk New St. Macroom.
Treasurer - Michael O'Keeffe, Grocer,
              New Street, Macroom.
The Executive Committee are
as follows :-

Stephen Connor, Blacksmith, New Street,
Macroom.

Charles Brown, Breadvandrios, New St,
Macroom.

Jeremiah Murphy, Carpenter, Main St,
Macroom,

Timothy Murphy, Carpenter, Main St,
Macroom,

James Murphy, Farmers Son mullenroe,
Macroom.

Patrick Donoghue, Farmers Son,
Carrignorthane, Macroom,

Daniel Harrington, Farmer, Knockeaham,
Macroom.

Michael Sullivan, med student,
Caherdahy, macroom,

John Lynch, Drapers Clerk, New St,
Macroom.

John Mullane, Drapers Clerk, New St
macroom,

John Long, Drapers Clerk, Main St,
macroom,

Henry Brown, Farmer, Raleigh,
Macroom.

(2) Denis Lynch, New Street, Macroom,
was selected to represent the Division
on the governing body of Sinn Fein.

(3) Denis Lynch, New Street Macroom,
was also selected as the Sinn Fein
Candidate for a Parliamentary
vacancy in the Division should

one arise. He is a draper & member
of the Macroom U.D. Council,
Prior to the inauguration of the Sinn
Fein movement he was an advanced
Hibernian & Nationalist & took an
active part in Parliamentary Elections.
He is now the principal Sinn Fein
leader in Macroom District. He is
always the principal speaker at
the local Sinn Fein meetings, & so
far does not appear to be a physical
force man. His great ambition
is to get elected M.P. for the
Division.

L. Sweeny

CI.

Proposed public Sinn Fein meeting at Ballinalee
On 7th October 1917

1 Has there been any previous Sinn Fein meeting If so with what result

Yes a public Sinn Fein meeting was held at Ballinalee on 25th July 1917 Thomas Ashe who spoke at the meeting was prosecuted Court martialled and sentenced to one years imprisonment He has died undergoing imprisonment

2 Are there any Grazing Farms in Your Sub Dist or Derelict or evicted farms taken by new tenant about which there might be trouble

No

3 Any boycotted obnoxious persons in Your Sub Dist or persons receiving police Protection

4 Any strange relations between Landlord and tenant or between master and servant in Your Sub Dist

5 Has there been any recent outrages or intimidation

6 If any placard re meeting has been posted send in a Copy if You Can

no placards has been posted up yet

7 Whether meeting is outdoor or indoor

Outdoor

Lastly any other information which You know should be given

It has not Yet been decided whether the meeting will be held on the public Street of Ballinalee or in a field convenient to the village

Thomas R Byrne Con 55960
for Sgt Keich.

The Dist Inspector

Proposed public Sinn Fein meeting at Ballinalee on 7th October 1917

County of Longford

Ballinalee 28th September 1917

I beg to report that arrangements are being made for the holding of a Sinn Fein public meeting at Ballinalee on Sunday 7th October next The meeting is expected to be a large one as contingents are expected from all parts of the County I am informed that Joseph Maguinness Sinn Fein M P for South Longford and his brother Francis Maguinness J.P. Longford has promised to address the meeting The meeting has been announced in a paragraph of the Roscommon Herald of 22nd inst but no posters have yet been put up in this Sub Dist- I attach cutting above referred to and other speakers are also invited As this is the place where Mr Thomas Ashe made the speech for which he was awarded one year's imprisonment and now dead In consequence of this I expect there will be speeches of a strong seditious nature and would respectfully suggest that a government notetaker be sent to take notes of the speeches delivered I would also suggest that an extra force of about 20 Men be sent to preserve the peace If posters are displayed I will send in a copy later on

Thomas R Byers Con 55960 for Sgt Sich

The Dist Inspector

GRANARD 29th Sept 1917.

Submitted. I beg to attach copy of posters several of which are

THE COUNTY INSPECTOR.

displayed in shop windows in Groward.

I do not anticipate any disturbance
at the meeting, but if the persons
named attend, it is probable that
seditious language will be used,
and it would be advisable to have a
shorthand writer present. The people
in the locality are generally well disposed.
I suggest that twenty extra men should
be sent in the event of a shorthand
note-taker attending. Should a shorthand writer not be sent, two local
men could be told off to take mental
notes, and an extra force of twelve
men would be sufficient to preserve
the peace. I could supply fifteen
extra men from this District,

Chas. Collins

2 S.I.

38 S.   Crime Special
83244

Proposed public Sinn Fein meeting at
Ballinalee on 7th October 1917.

SECRET.

COUNTY OF Longford

County Inspector's Office,
Longford 30 Sept 1917.

C.I. Longford.

A. Mental
notes of any
illegal language
will suffice.
Please report
as soon as
possible after
the meeting

J Kirkholmes A
C.I.
for I.G.

5/10/17

Submitted; a Sinn Fein public meeting
is to be held at Ballinalee on Sunday
October 7th. As Ballinalee is the village
where the late Thomas Ashe made the seditious
speech, and where the two Constables who took
the notes are still stationed; the matter
will no doubt be referred to in any speeches.
However I don't anticipate any trouble —
If a shorthand note taker is deemed to be
necessary an extra force of 20 men would be
required. But if not. I will direct two
men to take mental notes. and I will
assemble a sufficient force from this
County. The speakers named in poster (attached)
are fairly important. I have no doubt
Darrell Figgis & Mr. Collins if they attend will
use fairly strong language and make
the occasion a somewhat dramatic one

The Insp General

owing to the fact that the seditious
(asked)
speech which led to his death was
made at Ballinalee ———

Beyond the dramatic side of the meeting
I dont anticipate any trouble '

         Regards Heard
                 CI

SECRET.   COUNTY OF Longford
                 ....

       County Inspector's Office,
         Longford. 6ᵗ Oct 19 17

For your information : As directed
Two men will take mental notes . Report
as soon as possible .

              Regards Heard
                   CI

The D.I. Granard

Notes taken by Const. Thos Joseph.

Sinn Fein Meeting at Ballinalee 7:10:1917

County Of Longford
Ballinalee 8:10:1917

I beg to report I attended a Sinn Fein meeting in
Ballinalee on 7:10:1917 accompanied by Sergt Casey.
Rev P. Markey P.P. Clonbroney was appointed chairman
and addressed the meeting and said He was proud to
see such a crowd present before him that day
He reffered to the lamented death of poor Thomas Ashe
who addressed them here not long ago. and was
arrested and tried by Court Marshal in
Dublin You all know the rest may his soul rest
in peace. — The Irish party were only a fraud
the were usless. So join the Sinn Fein movement you know what it is now & pleas God
we will have a free & United Ireland from sea to sea
Joseph McGuinness M.P.
Addressed them in Irish for some time. and after
He refferred to the lamented death of poor Thomas Ashe
who was amongst You here only a few months ago
where He made his last speach in Ballinalee and
was sent to Imprisonment where he met his fate
He told the people of North Longford to join the
Sinn Fein Clubs. and as the days were getting
short now. thy would not be able to have
many more large Demonstrations like this for some-
time He said the Could organise in the Clubs or
their own houses it was by organisation the
seats in South Longford Roscommon Clare and
Kilkenny were won and organisation that
will win all the seats that will become vacant
in Ireland. He referred to the late Father Tom Conefry
Killoe & Father Pinkman Newtowncashel as a loss to Sinn Fein
the latter gave valuable assistance at South Longford Election
The Sergt.

James Oneil Ballinamuck

addressed the meeting and said He was a long
time connected with the National movement and
owing to knowing it so well it was nothing but
a fraud all trickery and doggery the Irish members
doom was sealed and written on the walls of
Westminister and his resignation was read
from the Parlimentry Party was read by John Walsh.

"Captain" Collins

addressed them in Irish —   He then referred to
the death of Thomas Ashe who he said he was with
the night he made his last speech here. from
which speech. he was sent to Kilmanem
Gaol where he died and two Police that gave
evedence which was contradictory as he would
explain to them those two did not swear the
truth. one swore one thing & the othe. contradicted him with reference to a despatch
from Pierce to Ashe before his execution
Ashe died and what he died for should be
carried out, and from what I have seen
before me here today they would win
a free & united Nation.   Ths. Ashe is not
dead his Spirit is still with us if he
could only speak and appear. He explained
to them the need for organisation and if
the did that the would have no trouble
in putting their case before the peace Conference
when the war was over and as some one
had said nothing would be got from
England unless you approach them with
the head of a Landlord in one hand and the
tail of a Bullock in the other.

Thomas Finlan Edgeworthstown
addressed the meeting and denounced the Irish
party. and their way of going on and told
all to join the Sinn Fein movement it was
the only means of freeing Ireland

P. D. Cusack. Granard.
addressed the meeting by returning thanks to
them for the great reception the gave him
appearing in Uniform and said he would
like to see every one around him wearing the
same uniform he told them to organise and
keep their Sinn Fein clubs in good working
order in North Longford

Patrick McCarty Bunlahy
Proposed a vote of thanks to Rev P. Markey for
presiding at the meeting and said it was
a good sign of the times to see the priest and
people on the same platform.

F. McGuinness JP. Longford
In Seconding the vote of thanks Said he was
sorry he was not called on sooner as he intended
referring to a matter which he would not do now
He referred to the death of Thomas Ashe and
how the case was made out against him by those
who supplied the report of his speech and he
hoped that North Longford would strike a
blow when the time would come against those
who supplied the information. He also said that
Joseph Deane Said Sinn Fein should be put down.
                    Thomas Joseph
                    Const. 59198.

Notes taken by Sgt. M. Casey, Ballinala

Resolutions read by J. Walsh

I That we call on the member of Parliament for
north Longford to resign his seat in Parliament
as he no longer represents the people of
north Longford

II That we condemn the treatment of Irish
political prisoners, and that copies of this resolution
be sent to the President of the U.S. America &
other allied nations, and to point out the attitude
of the Government towards political prisoners in this
country as compared with their attitude towards
those who commit similar crimes in Russia

The Rev. P. Markey P.P. addressed the meeting and said
he congratulated them on the large number of people
present. He referred to the death of the lamented
late Thos. Ashe, who addressed there only a few
months ago. He spoke about the Irish Parliamentary
Party and said they were useless and only a fraud.
He asked the people to join the Sein Fein movement &
that in time they would have a free & united Ireland
from sea to sea in Ireland.

Joe McGuinness M.P. addressed the meeting & at
first spoke in Irish. He then referred to the late
T. Ashe, who made his last public speech in
Ballinalee, for which he was sentenced to imprisonment
in Mountjoy Gaol, where he met his death, through
the hands of the British Government. He advised those
present to join the Sein Fein movement and to form

form

Sein Fein Clubs and to get organised and that
they could do this in their club rooms and in their
homes. He said that in future they would not be
able to have many big public meetings like this,
as the days would be getting short. He referred
the Sein Fein victories in Roscommon, Longford,
Clare & Kilkenny and said when the opportunity
offered they would win every seat in Ireland,
and then would have the Irish Parliamentary Party, who
were so false to the country, banished for ever.

He said the deaths of the late Rev. Frs. Pinkman
& Honefoy were a big loss to the Sein Fein
movement in this county.

James Oneill C Councillor, addressed the meeting
and told how long he was connected with the
national movement, and that owing to the
treachery & meanness of the Irish Parliamentary Party, he became
a Sein Feiner and asked that his resignation from
the U.I.L. be read to the meeting, which was
done by J. Walsh

Capt Collins, addressed the meeting & spoke at
first in Irish. He then referred to the death of the
late Thos Ashe. and said he was there with Ashe
the day he made his last speech there, for which
he was sent to Gaol and died. He said he would tell
them how Ashe was convicted and sent to Gaol & died.
He said the first of it was that he made a speech
there, which was reported by two Police who were at the
meeting. Those Police did not (he said) swear the truth

truth

Collins's Continued

He said he was present and heard what ashe
had said. He said one of the Police contradicted the
other, with reference to a statement made by ashe, about
the alleged conveyance of a despatch from the
late Rebel leader - Pierce - to ashe, before. Pierce's
execution. He said the cause for which ash died
for should be carried on until they had won, and
he was sure from what he saw there, that they would
carry on the fight. He said that although ash was
dead that his spirit remained. He told them all
to organise and join the sein Fein movement, and
that their case would be put before the Peace
Conference when the war was over. He wound
up his speech by quoting from some men who
said long ago that "You will not get anything from
the British Government unless you approach them
with a bullock's tail in one hand and a
landlord's head in the other."

J. Finlow addressed the meeting and condemned the
Irish Parliamentary Party and their methods, and
asked those present to join the Sein Fein movement.

Paul Busack. appeared in the uniform of the Irish Volunteer.
He said I am glad you all admire my uniform.
You should be all wearing the same uniform.
Let you all organise and be one body.

Pat McCarthy proposed a vote of thanks to Father
Markey for presiding at the meeting

meeting

J. McGuinness J.P. seconded the vote of thanks
to Father Markey, and said he was sorry he
was not called earlier as he intends referring
to a matter which he would refer to at a future
date. He referred to how the case was made
against Thos. Ashe by those political hucksters
who supplied the report of his speech, and he
hoped that when the time came that north
Longford would strike a blow at those who
supplied the report of Ashe's speech. (This appears
to be directed to J.P. Farrell M.P. who reported the
speech in the "Longford Leader"). Mr McGuinness
then referred to Joe Dare of Longford as having
said in Ballinalee on 16th Sept 17 that the Government
should put down the Sinn Feiners

M. Casey Sergt 32810

Crime Special

Sinn Fein meeting at Ballinalee Village
on Sunday. 7th inst. —

SECRET.

[stamp: R.I. CONSTABULARY / Received / 8 OCT 1917 / Dublin Castle / CRIME SPE]

COUNTY OF Longford.

County Inspector's Office,

Longford. 8th Oct. 1917

With reference to C.S. File $\frac{38}{83244}$ S. 5. 10. 17. at

present with S.I. at Granard I beg to report briefly
(as original reports with notes re cannot reach me
till. tomorrow) that all passed off quietly
at the Sinn Fein meeting at Ballinalee on
yesterday — the holding of an Aeridheacht was
abandoned owing to the weather. but a public meeting
was held in the village of Ballinalee —

The following speakers addressed the meeting
Rev. Fr Markey P.P. presided - who spoke. Joseph
McGuinness M.P. - Michael Collins. Dublin
Francis McGuinness J.P., Thos. Fenlon. Paul D. Cusack
& other local men. — Prior to the meeting a
parade was held through the village. marching
in fours. P. D. Cusack wore Volunteer uniform as did
two others from Granard — About 1000 were
present. which included contingents from Gowna (Cavan)
Lanesboro. Longford Town — Clonguish or with 5 or 6
bands — The speeches were of the usual Sinn
Fein type — Collins making the principal speech referring
to the Ashe case — Full report will be submitted
as soon as possible. In all about 20 men were present.

R. Esquell Head Ct

The Inspector General

314 p
646   Crime Special.

Suspect Michael Collins Dublin.

County of Longford.
Granard 22·10·17.

I beg to report that above named
suspect arrived here alone on Saturday night
20th inst., for the Columbkille Aeridheacht, and
put up at the Greville Arms Hotel. He left for
Columbkille about 2½ p.m. on Sunday 21st inst.
accompanied by Paul D. Cusack and John Cawley
Granard, and they returned again to Granard
about 8 p.m. Collins left this morning for
Dublin travelling by the 9·33 a.m. train from
Ballywillan. I attach copy of cipher
telegram sent to the D.M.P.

Collins is well known here and he spent
most of his time with Cusack + Cawley and
other Sinn Feiners but he kept in and about
the Hotel and did not attend any meeting or
other assembly in Granard.

M. Lang Sgt. 56232

The Dist. Inspector,
GRANARD 22nd Oct. 19 17
Submitted.
Chas. Collins
2 D.I.

THE COUNTY INSPECTOR.

A °

Prefix _____ Code _____

POST OFFICE TELEGRAPHS.
(Inland Official Telegrams only.)

No. of Telegram _____

Office of Origin and Service Instructions.	Words.	Sent
Q. H. M. S.		At _____ .M.
Handekin 10·40 *a.m.*		To _____
22 : 10 : 17.		By _____

I certify that this Telegram is sent on the service of the

R. I. Constabulary

(Signature) *M. Lang Sgt.*

Attention is called to the Regulations printed at the back hereof.

Dated Stamp.

TO: *Camp Dublin*

By 9·33 a.m. train from Ballywillan to Broadstone Suspect Michael Collins Dublin

FROM: *Sergeant Constabulary Granard*

he **Name and Address of the Sender, IF NOT TO BE TELEGRAPHED,** should be written in the Space provided at the Back of the Form.

(6779) Wt. 28653-3044. 450,000. 12/10. Wy. & S., Ltd **Sch. 49.**

Confidential

Coof Longford

Lanesboro 22 : 2 : 18

Assault in Sinn Fein Hall in Tullyvrane

I beg to report that on last night at a
meeting of Sinn Fein and Irish Volunteers in the hall
in Tullyvrane. Alfred Kemp son of Ex Con Kemp
attended to be enrolled as a Volunteer. Patrick
Clyne who is in charge of the Volunteers brought
Kemp into the hall and told him to fall in with
the rest of the Volunteers. Michael J. Ryan
objected, that Kemp should fall in, without the
usual questions been put to him, and the usual
formalities gone through with Kemp same as
when enrolling others. The result being that some
angry words occurred between Clyne & Ryan. the
latter calling Clyne a grabber. Clyne then struck
Ryan with a stick and partly stunned him.
Clyne then left the hall, but returned and
ordered the Volunteers to fall in for a route march
the volunteers fell in in different groups and
would not obey any person. I was speaking to
Ryan today he will take no proceedings
against Clyne, as it would throw discredit
on the movement. The route march did not take
place, and it is expected that this occurrence
will cause a split in the Volunteer movement
here. Consts Kearney & Duffy were in the
vicinity of the hall.

The Dist Inspr   J. J. Foley
    Longford.   Sergt 57760

Secret   Crime Special

County of Longford

Lanesboro 3 : 3 : 18

Court-Martial in Tullyvrane Sinn Fein Hall.

           I beg to report that at 6 pm on 2nd Inst. ~ Collins Sinn Fein organiser Dublin arrived here to hold a Court-Martial in above hall, on Patrick Clyne Captain I. Volunteers charged with assaulting Michael I. Ryan 1st Lieut. At 7½ pm the Ratheline Volunteers assembled at the hall, and the proceedings commenced inside locked doors ~ Collins presiding.

           After evidence been taken the following decision was given :- Captain Clyne & Lieut Ryan to be reduced to the ranks of Private for six months, at the end of that time their case would be further considered.

           The following promotions were then made.

I.   Thomas Gibbons. Clonflower. Adjutant

II. Francis Clarke. Lanesboro. 1st Lieut.

III. Patrick I. McCcrann, Jr. Do 2nd Lieut.

IV. Thomas McDermott. Mountdavys. Quarter master.

No Captain being appointed in Clyne place.

           At 9¼ pm. the Cloontuskert Volunteers 24 in number marching in fours arrived at the hall. they would not be allowed to enter until the inquiry was over. At 9½ pm. they were admitted when some military exercise was gone through. I saw through a window two men fencing with hurleys. After the exercise a speech was given presumably by Collins, there being great clapping of hands at intervals. At 10½ pm all left the Dist Sraper

left the hall. Francis Clarke ordered the
Volunteers to fall in two deep, in this formation
they marched about 200 yards, when they were
halted, numbered & formed in fours. They
then marched to beside the barracks singing
the Soldiers song. where they were halted
and dismissed. They then broke away and
dispersed quietly. There were 56 Volunteers
on parade followed by a crowd of 50 people
It being so dark we could not identify any of
them except by their voice. Collins left here
at 11¾ pm to Longford to meet some other person
there. I am of the opinion that the split is not
healed yet. Clynes followers will cause further
trouble in the ranks, and some of them refused
to fall in on parade when called on.

                                        John J. Foley
                                        Cc 51746
Longford. 5. 3. 18.
          Submitted.
               E.E. Purtin 102

The Co. Insp.

SECRET.   COUNTY OF Longford

          County Inspector's Office,
               Longford 6 March 1918.

Submitted for information. Michael Collins is very
active lately in this Co. and is working up this
Irish Volunteers movement —

                                   Reginald Heard
                                        CI

The Insp. Gen.

18482 SECRET.

$$\frac{38}{5000} \text{ S.}$$

ROYAL IRISH CONSTABULARY OFFICE, DUBLIN CASTLE.

Crime Department— Special Branch

(The Officer to whom this File is addressed is responsible for its safe custody.)

SUBJECT _Irish Volunteers at Lanesboro' Co Longford._
Court martial on Volunteers . Michael Collins of Dublin.

Date _____ 7. March _____ 1918

I.S.

Submitted for information.

On 21/2/18 – the Captain knocked down the 1st Lieut. with a stick in the Volunteer Hall.

A courtmartial was held on 2/3/18, & both officers were reduced to the ranks.

Michael Collins of Dublin conducted the trial. He is said to be a leading man in the Irish Volunteer Executive in Dublin.

He addressed a meeting at Ballinamuck near Granard on 17/2/18 & drilled 40 Volunteers.

He has been paying attention to Co Longford.

J. Byrne

Under Secretary

2.9.

Submitted. It is assumed that the Police have no evidence of this holding of this Court Martial & that Ryan who discussed the assault with Sergt Foley would not give evidence.

W.M.B. 8/3

Seen.
W.N.B. 8/3

I.G.
RETURNED
8 MAR 1918

W.4779.70.5000.10/17/A.P.Co.,Ltd.   8786.

Crime special

Sinn Fein Demonstration at Ballinamuck
Report from Mental Notes.

Co. of Longford

Ballinamuck J.C. 17: 2: 1918

I beg to report that a Sinn Fein meeting
was held here after mass about 300 attended
James Brady Secretary of local Sinn F. C.
introduced James O'Neill crowdrummin farmer
and Co. Councillor, who addressed the meeting
he thanked the people for attending there
that day in such large numbers, he
criticised the action of the Irish Party generally
and advised the young men of Ballinamuck
to join Sinn Fein & Irish volunteers, and to
be ready in a few months time for the independence of Ireland which would come as a
result of the peace conference. He said there
was no trust in British Ministers, & therefore
it was useless to send members to the British
House of Commons. John Redmond three
years ago wanted the young men to join an
Irish Regiment to be sent to the war to
be slaughtered and buried in pits in France
Let the Government deliver the goods and
the Irish people would be as loyal as
any other people in the world.

James Brady See. local S.F.C. read the
following resolutions. (1) That we the members
of Ballinamuck S.F.C. call on J.P. Farrell
temporary member for N. Longford to resign
as he no longer represents the majority
of people in this constituency. (2) That we
call on all the young men of this parish
to at once join the Sinn Fein Club and
Irish volunteers. (3) That we condemn
the action of the Nationalists of S. Armagh
for the tactics used by them at the By Election
and in joining the unholy alliance
with the unionists and cursing the Pope

The Sgt

"Captain Collins" was then introduced and said he was glad to see such a fine crowd of young people, he advised all over 18 years to join the Irish Volunteers and get to work in earnest to be ready for self independence, he told them to drill & be prepared to assert their rights when the time came, the Convention had failed and it was now up to the Irish people to decide whether they were going to demand independence or remain a vassal state of John Bull. Books had been issued to each S.F.C. to take a plebiscite of all young men of over 18 years he hoped all would do so when asked by the Irish Volunteers, subscribe their names and in a month's time have their case ready for the peace conference

Ireland was being crushed by taxation, by independence Ireland could have her own Army & Navy some might say she was too poor & could not do anything of the sort. I say that in three years her revenue could build 10 Submarines then they would make England keep her Dreadnaughts Super-Dreadnaughts in their own Ports where the Quadruple Alliance's were keeping them at present as to the food he told them to keep it and not have another 47 over again then independence would not be much good to them

After the meeting he drilled 40 Irish Volunteers on the ball alley, numbered gave them form fours left & right, and marched them on about 50 yds & back again he explained to them how to keep their dressing and paces to be taken in formation of fours &c

Paul Dawson ~~Cusack~~ Granard advised
the men + women to join Sinn Fein
as the women would help too, for without
them they could not get along, old
and young to get to work without any
hesitation and join S.F. + Irish Volunteers
as it was the only movement by which
anything could be achieved at present
he also referred to the Irish Party and
how they carried out the contest at
South Armagh, the propaganda of the
Freeman, + Sco. good Leader, and how
the conduct of back lane people was
allowed to prevail at Electioneering
meetings.

Mr. Cawley, Granard, said he did
not wish to keep the people standing too
long with cold feet, but, in a good cause
they did not mind how long they stood
or what sacrifices they made, he told the
young men to join Sinn Fein + the Irish
volunteers, and show to the world that
they were determined to acquire a measure
of freedom for Ireland, every young
man who did not join the Irish volunteers
was a traitor, the young men of Ireland
should be ready to defeat conscription
and warned the people that the danger
was not yet over + that recently when
it had been brought up in Westminster
there were only 6 or 7 so called members
of the Irish party present to do what they
were well paid for doing for people whom
they pretended to represent.
                    Sgt McNabola
                                    Hugh Maguire, Constable
                                            59496
            Ballivamuck 18. 2. 1918
                    submitted
                    James Murhola, 453829
L D. I. Inspector

Crime Special

Re Sinn Fein Flags Processions and
Drilling

County of Longford

Ballinamuck Jo 17, 3, 1918

I beg to report for the information of the
C, M, A. that a Sinn Fein meeting was held
at Ballinamuck after mass about 11 am, on this date there
was one ordinary Sinn Fein Flag displayed
at the meeting by the side of the speaker.
after James O'Neill of Crowdrumin, Mr Collins
of Dublin introduced as Captain the Lewes
Prisioner, James Brady of Gaigue. Paul Dawson
Cussack, and John Cawley of Granard,
& Joseph Maguire of Legga addressed the
meeting on the sinn Fein & volunteer principals,
to about 200 people who came out from
Divine Service,

John & O'Neill of Crowdrumin farmers Son one
age 30 this sub District put 40 young men
through Drill movements ordered them to
form two Deep & Number then from the right,
and gave them form fours & after Captain
Collins Drilled them John & O'Neill dismissed
them and told them to salute after being Dismissed,
they were then Dismissed & some of them saluted,
Captain Collins Drilled those 40 young men and
numberd them twice and showed them how
to form fours & the turnings and to make time
he then gave them form fours. Right (front) & form
fours left (front) those were the Commands used,
and marched them down the Road for about
50 yards giving them left wheel, about turn.
Right wheel, and marched them to where
they started from, when John O'Neill Dismissed
them. Captain Collins warned them to make these
moves right and not having these Gentlemen
referring to the Police laughing at you, the Drill Movements
occupied about 10 minutes from 12 ½ to about 12 5/5 Pm. he then
went with them into a vacant house & closed the Door, & remained
there for about ½ an hour, everything passed off quiet, saw the Galley,
the Dist Inspector   James McGabola sgt 53829

COUNTY OF *Longford*

County Inspector's Office,
Longford 6th March 1918

Submitted for information. —
Michael Collins is visiting this locality
every much of late & working up the
Volunteer Movement. I am afraid his
influence if unchecked will have a
bad effect —

The D.I. full —   Reginald Heard
                                            C.I.

Sinn Fein meeting at Segga
Report of mental notes taken

Co. of Longford

Ballinamuck Jp. 4 : 3 : 1918

I beg to report that Captain Michael Collins Dublin, addressed a Sinn Fein meeting at Segga Chapel after 12 Oc masson yesterday He said that he didnt know much about speechmaking but, that he knew a little about the working of the G. P. O. in Easter week, he referred to the convention that it was not represented by the Irish people. It was rigged by Lloyd George and it was doomed to failure. The British Govnt. had no intention of giving them control of Customs, Excise, Judiciary or Police, consequently it would be worse than that attempted at the partition scheme. In S. Armagh though we were defeated we claim it as a victory for us. The Orangemen voted to a man for Donnelly the followers of the Allies, he said he was in a place in Armagh at the Election and he heard there were 150 Ulster volunteers there & that during Easter week when wild rumours were abroad that the South & west had joined the rebellion, those 150 U. V. went by night and gave in their arms & ammunition at the hall fearing they would have to fight the rebels. He said Sheridanism was now rampant in Co. Clare & other places in Ireland the old set were at work again trying to discredit their orgaisation he wished Longford and every county in Ireland was like Clare today that every little village in it was occupied by military with artillery armoured cars & machine guns

Sgt McNabola

He said Captain Murray of the Irish volunteers
was shot down by the Police and that they
ordered they people to stand aside till
they would finish him He said he
had a communication which their
organisation sent to the Press but the
latter part was censored and that
it would not be censored there that day

by the people of Moyne & Drumard
(1) That we the Irish volunteers warn
our members not to take part in raids
for arms useless old shotguns, swords,
especially from their friends & countrymen
(2) That we condemn the action of the Irish
volunteers for taking part in cattle drives
(3) That when volunteers do raid for arms
they will go where they will find ones
that will be of some use to them, and
that we call on the Irish volunteers to
defend their arms unto the death.
    The British Government was at their
wits end now about the man-power question
of the Empire. Ireland too was thinking
about her man-power emigration had
ceased for the past few years & it had
increased considerably. The Irish Party
claimed to have defeated conscription
but he claimed it was the men of Easter week
who had defeated it. The Cabinet might
attempt it again but it would take five
soldiers to take one man and 50,000
    with fixed bayonets to enforce it in Ireland
he would say to the Irish volunteers if such
was attempted to stand together & remember
Thomas Ash.
                        Hugh Maguire Con 59496

Ballbramed Jo 4.3.18
        sub mitted
            James Herabold
                        Sgt 528 39
District Inspector

Sinn Fein meeting at Legga
Report of mental notes taken
Co. of Longford
Ballinamuck Jb. 4 : 3 : 1918

I beg to report that Paul A. Cusack Granard
addressed a Sinn F. meeting at Legga they
after last mass 12 noon on yesterday
He said he could not understand why
any of they men of Moyne or Drumard
were not joining the ranks of Sinn Fein
that they must be fools or idiots to be
still believing in the Nationalist movement
that the Irish Party were doing nothing
for them only breakfasting with Lloyd George
and drawing their £400 a year the idea
of England proclaiming to the world that
she was advocating the cause of small nations
but not a word about poor old Ireland or self
determination. India & Egypt were
invaded by England for their protection &
there she remains Ireland too was invaded
and here she remains but our case would
go before the peace conference, Dr. MᶜCartan
who was turned down by S. Armagh
worked his way to america as a stoker
shovelling coal + is now in the embassy
at Washington where the volunteers paid
£400 for a house for him where the tricolour
flag waves over it. Russia & america
was on their side. England would
not acknowledge the Bolcheviks of Russia
after the revolution. No she is not now going
to give the knock out blow to the enemy
I may tell you that she is not winning
that she is down + out in this war
+ we are sorry for the poor old Empire

Sgt. _____   Hugh Maguire Leon
Ballinmuck Jb 4, 3/8   59496
      submitted
The Sub Inspector   Jam. Numbols 4,4.5,78,9

19373

99

Drilling by Sinn Feiners

D. R. Reg. 9 Tr. and Military Exercises and Drill
Order

CHIEF SECRETARY'S
7017
9 MAR 1918
OFFICE

R.I. CONSTABULARY OFFICE
Received
MAR 1918
Dublin

Sergt

Ballinrobe Co. [?] 3. 3. 18

I beg to report for the information of the
C.M.A. that while on duty accompanied
by Const. Maguire after a Sinn Fein
meeting held on the 3d inst. at [?] Ga
Chapel Mr. Collins age 35 of Dublin
fell in 88 young men on the public Road
and drilled them for about ½ of an
hour. he numbered them off from
the right on two occasions and
showed them how to form fours,
and gave them form fours, right
quick march down about 100 yards
the Road & halted them, and gave them
front and explained how they were
to come up to their places and check the
heels like the Prussians after marching
them up and down the Road three times
he dismissed them and told them
how to salute with the right hand &
Mr. Paul Dawson Cusack of [?] of the
age about 35 assisted Mr. Collins in pulling
them into fours by taking them by the
shoulders and he then went up the Road
about 200 yards as from the meeting
place & drilled 20 young men & gave
them form fours & till resumed
them he gave them this Drill under
the supervision of Mr. Collins

James Kimbole Sergt 53929

I think this
man should be
brought to Dublin
by C.M.A.
tried in Dublin
on a charge

This man should
be arrested charged
before a C.M. in
with intent
to avoid forums
[?] forward
for trial
meanwhile
[?]

8.3.18

Act accordingly Head Constable & Inspector
W. P. B.

"Re Sinn Fein meeting at Legga
&c Mental notes taken on 3.3.18

County of Longford

Ballinamuck Jr 3. 3. 1918

I beg to report that at a Sinn Fein meeting held
at Legga chapel this sub Dist on this date
after 11 oclock Mass I took the following mental
notes of the speeches,

" Mr Michael Collins of Dublin who was introduced
by Mr Joseph Maguire, He was there that Day
for business the same as when he worked
in the post office in Dublin Easter week,
He read from a piece of paper the orders of
the Executive (1) which said they were against
the Raids (2) against Cattle Driving
(3) which was not past by Censor but which

A. {

would be passed thro', They advised the
volunteers not to take old swords or shot guns
from fellow neighbours, but what they
wanted was rifles, and they knew where
to get them, and advised the volunteers
to hold their rifles when they got them,
and defend themselves till death,
and denied that the volunteers were getting
up those Raids, but like always the
government was at the Back of it, and
like Sheridan, they wanted to show up the
country as doing those things, he referred
to the Armagh Election and the Class of Home
Rule Ireland was getting & referred to the
military in Clare and advised them in this
county to Do like Clare
and as for Conscription he told them it would
take five men to bring one of them that was
there, and if they put on Conscription he said
to them Remember Ashe,

" Mr Paul Dawson Cussack of Garrad was then
introduced He then addressed the people and
referred to John Redmond Dillon Devlin & P Farrell
as a bad famed lot, he said that Sinn Fein volunteers
were the right aide,

were the right side

And to march under that flag
he referred to the war & John Redmond
and other members advising them to put
up a fight on the western front, and referred
to English rule and told them how they
come over to Ireland for a while but
ye all know they stopped in it, and
advised them there that day to put up
the fight, at the next general election
in this county on the western front, put in
a proper man to Represent them as that.
was the flag pointing to a Sinn Fein flag
for them to follow,

James Merabole Sgt 53829

Secret. Crime Special.

Sinn Fein Meeting at Legga,
Ballinamuck, subdist. on 3rd March, 1918.

COUNTY OF LONGFORD.

GRANARD 5th March 1918

I beg to report that a public Sinn
Fein meeting was held outside Legga
Chapel after second Mass on 3rd inst.

About 300 persons, with two bands were
present. Joseph Maguire of Legga acted as
chairman, and the only speakers were
Michael Collins Dublin, member of the
Sinn Fein Council, and Paul D. Cusack
of Granard. The meeting was not publicly
announced, but the Sergeant from
Ballinamuck had got word of it and
was in attendance with a Constable.
Two Constables from Arva also
attended with a band and contingent
from that subdistrict.

The language was seditious, and intended
to cause disaffection. Collins' remarks
at A in Sergt. Mc Nabola's report seem
to be a direct incentive to rob the Police
of their rifles. So far as is known there
are no other rifles in the subdistrict.

After the meeting Collins and Cusack
drilled 88 of the party on the road.
Copies of mental notes made by Sergt.
Mc Nabola and Const. Maguire are annexed.

Chas. Collins

THE COUNTY INSPECTOR.

GRANARD _5th March 19 18._

    Submitted. Michael Collins was reported to the C.M.A. for drilling at Ballinamuck on 17th Ult. He appears to be a very dangerous criminal, is a member of the Sinn Féin Council, and boasts about the part he took in capturing the G.P.O. He has paid frequent visits to this District, and his activities, if not speedily restrained, will lead to serious mischief.

    No weapons were carried on this occasion. I submit a separate report for the information of the C.M.A.

Chas. Collins
S.I.

THE COUNTY INSPECTOR.

COUNTY OF _Longford_

County Inspector's Office,

Longford 6 March 1918

    Submitted. After the Sinn Féin meeting at Legga chapel on 3 March Michael Collins drilled 88 men assisted by Paul & Rusnell of Granard — no uniform was worn or arms carried —

Reginald Beauf
C.I.

The Inspector General

I. Office - note.

1937 3

II C.I. Longford

For compliance with the attorney Generals minute.

An Information should be sworn before the R. M. against Collins & a warrant obtained for his arrest.

When he has been arrested he should be returned for trial to assizes on a charge of incitement to raid for arms.

The R.M. should be requested to require Collins to find sureties of the peace & good behaviour pending his trial at assizes.

Inform the C.M.A.

D+G

11. 3. 18.

COUNTY OF Longford

County Inspector's Office,

Longford 12 March 19 18

For compliance please. Do you know the address of Michael Collins in Dublin? I have informed C.M.A

E.S.Prostin

County Inspector, R. I. Constabulary.

D. Granard.

GRANARD 4th Apl. 1918.

I beg to state that Collins lodged at 44 Mountjoy St. Dublin.

A warrant was obtained as directed and sent to the D.M.P. for execution. Collins was arrested in Dublin on 2nd Inst. and on the following morning he was conveyed to Longford, and brought before Mr Jephson R.M. who took Depositions and returned the accused for trial to the next Assizes for the County. The accused, who was very abusive and insulting, refused to recognize the court or to give bail, and was removed to Sligo gaol.

He admitted the truth of the Police evidence.

Chas. Collins
Sgt.

COUNTY OF Longford
....

County Inspector's Office,

Longford 5 April 1918.

Submitted. I beg to state that I have informed C.M.d of result of proceedings so far.

Reynell Sheaf
County Inspector,
R.I. Constabulary.

The Inspr General.

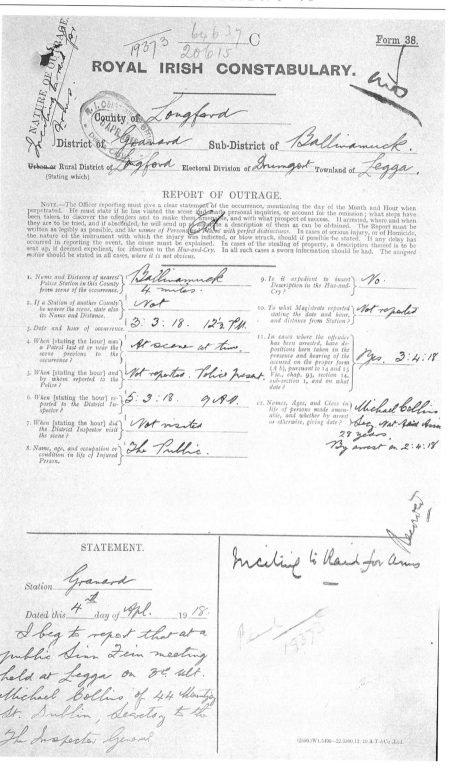

64637 C
19373
20615

Form 38.

ROYAL IRISH CONSTABULARY.

NATURE OF OUTRAGE.

County of *Longford*

District of *Granard*   Sub-District of *Ballinamuck.*

Urban or Rural District of *Longford*   Electoral Division of *Drumgort* Townland of *Legga.*
(Stating which)

REPORT OF OUTRAGE.

NOTE.—The Officer reporting must give a clear statement of the occurrence, mentioning the day of the Month and Hour when perpetrated. He must state if he has visited the scene and made personal inquiries, or account for the omission; what steps have been taken to discover the offenders and to make them amenable, and with what prospect of success. If arrested, where and when they are to be tried, and if absconded, he will send up as accurate a description of them as can be obtained. The Report must be written as legibly as possible, and *the names of Persons and Places with perfect distinctness.* In cases of serious injury, or of Homicide, the nature of the instrument with which the injury was inflicted, or blow struck, should if possible be stated. If any delay has occurred in reporting the event, the cause must be explained. In cases of the stealing of property, a description thereof is to be sent up, if deemed expedient, for insertion in the *Hue-and-Cry.* In all such cases a sworn information should be had. The assigned *motive* should be stated in all cases, *where it is not obvious.*

1. Name and Distance of nearest Police Station in this County from scene of the occurrence. | *Ballinamuck 4 miles.*
2. If a Station of another County be nearer the scene, state also its Name and Distance. | *Not*
3. Date and hour of occurrence. | *3: 3: 18 - 12½ P.M.*
4. When [stating the hour] was a Patrol last at or near the scene previous to the occurrence? | *At scene at time*
5. When [stating the hour] and by whom reported to the Police? | *Not reported. Police present.*
6. When [stating the hour] reported to the District Inspector? | *5. 3. 18. 9 A.M.*
7. When [stating the hour] did the District Inspector visit the scene? | *Not visited*
8. Name, age, and occupation or condition in life of Injured Person. | *The Public.*

9. Is it expedient to insert Description in the Hue-and-Cry? | *No.*
10. To what Magistrate reported stating the date and hour, and distance from Station? | *Not reported*
11. In cases where the offender has been arrested, have depositions been taken in the presence and hearing of the accused on the proper form (A b), pursuant to 14 and 15 Vic., chap. 93, section 14, sub-section 1, and on what date? | *Yes. 3:4:18*
12. Names, Ages, and Class in life of persons made amenable, and whether by arrest or otherwise, giving date? | *Michael Collins Sec. Nat. Aid Assn 28 years. By arrest on 2:4:18*

STATEMENT.

Station *Granard*

Dated this *4th* day of *Apl.* 19*18.*

*I beg to report that at a
public Sinn Fein meeting
held at Legga on 3rd ult.
Michael Collins of 44 Mountjoy
St. Dublin, Secretary to the
The Inspector General*

Meeting to Raid for Arms

(2550.)W t.5400—22.3500.12/10.A.T.&Co.,Ltd.

Secret

$\frac{3/4}{6755}$ S

Suspect Michael Collins. No. 7. D.M.P.
war B List.

County of Sligo.

Sligo 24: 4: 18

C.C.D.M.P.

Transmitted
for information.

C.I. for I.G.

26/4

Supt. C. Divn.

C. Commr 27/4/18

The Inspector General,

Transmitted.

C. Commr 30/4/18   The Dist Inspt

I beg to report that
I am informed, that the above named suspect
was released from Sligo prison 22nd inst,
and left for Broadstone by 1.40 pm train
same date.

Collins was returned for trial at the Longford
P.S. on 3rd inst, for inciting others to raid for arms,
and was committed to prison. He has now
given bail to appear for trial at the next
Longford Assizes, and to keep the peace
and be of good behaviour.

Nothing was known about his release
on bail, until 23rd inst when immediate
inquiry was made. His release caused
caused no excitement & some prominent local
Sinn Feiners were not pleased, when he
gave bail. I am informed the men
who bailed him are from County Longford.
Collins was not adhered to D.m.P.

M Dolan
S. 49891

115.

Secret. $\frac{314}{1050}$ S°   Crime Special

Suspect Michael Collins, Dublin

COUNTY OF LONGFORD

GRANARD 23rd Apl. 1918.

I beg to report the above named
arrived in Granard by car at 6 P.M.
yesterday, coming apparently from the
direction of Edgeworthstown. His
coming was anticipated, as about
a quarter of an hour before his arrival
about sixty Sinn Feiners formed up
in two lines at extended order opposite
Kiernan's hotel to welcome him.

At being market day, a considerable
crowd collected with some Sinn Fein
flags and sang "The Soldier's Song".

Collins put up at the hotel where he
remained until 9 P.M., when he left for
Edgeworthstown on Kiernan's motor car,
evidently intending to travel by train
to Dublin.

About 80 Sinn Feiners formed up
opposite the hotel when he was leaving.
His departure was ciphered to the
D.M.P. this morning.

On 3rd Inst. Collins was returned
for trial to the next Longford Assizes

THE COUNTY INSPECTOR

on a charge of inciting to raid for arms.
He refused on that occasion to give
bail or to recognize the court, and
was removed to Sligo jail.

The fact that he has now entered
into bails may be taken as an
indication that the resistance to
conscription will not be merely passive.

                           Chas. Collins
                              2.S.T.

                          COUNTY OF Longford

SECRET.

County Inspector's Office,
         Longford 24. 4.   1918

Submitted, Per File 19373 / 11.3.18. This man
was returned for trial in custody for inciting to
raid for Arms & at the time refused to give bail
& was committed to Sligo Gaol unto Assizes
He has now given bail — His object is apparently
to be at large so that he can be more useful
to the Sinn Fein cause should any disturbance
arise .

                            Reynell Newell
                                CI

The Inp Genl

It is rumoured that Sinn Fein H. Qrs. has
arranged that all such prisoners may give
bail in future —
                           R.Th

Secret

Suspects Michl Collins &   Crime Special.
Paul D Cusack.

38 S
7385
S.
8260

County of Longford

R.I. CONSTABULARY OFFICE
Received
1 — JUN. 1918
Dublin Castle
CRIME SPECIAL BRANCH

Granard. 10.5.18

I beg to report that Suspects Michl Collins
and Paul D Cusack left Granard at 9½ pm
on 9th inst by motor for Streete Ry Station
and thence to Dublin by last train.
Collins attended 12 noon mass on 9th inst
(a R.C. Holiday) in Company with Cusack.
They were afterwards joined by suspect
John Cawley of Granard, and all three spent
about 2 hours at Cusacks house.
Except as stated Collins did not move
about very much on 9th inst. but remained at the Hotel the greater part of the
day. His movements on 8th inst have
been reported already. I ciphered particulars
to Damp today

Joseph Gallacher
Sgt. 55 9 3.

The Dist Inspr Granard.
GRANARD 10th May 1918.

Submitted. The report of this suspects
arrival in Granard was submitted
yesterday.

Chas. Collins.
D.I.

Secret

38
7385

Suspect Paul D. Cusack

Co of Longford

Granard. 12.5.18

I beg to report that the above-named suspect returned to Granard from Dublin. He arrived about 10.45 pm on 11th inst by cycle from the Floot direction. He accompanied Suspect Michl Collins to Dublin from Streete Ry Station on night of 9th inst by 10 pm train

J. Gallagher S 55713

D.I. Granard.
GRANARD 12th May. 1918.
Submitted.
Chas Collins
2 S.I.

THE COUNTY INSPECTOR.

SECRET.

County Inspector's Office,
Longford 13.5.18.

Submitted this Suspect went to Dublin with Michael Collins Dublin Suspect — No doubt in connection with some Sinn Fein or Anti-Conscription work — Report re Collins departure sent on 11.5.18

R Sypull Head

$\frac{219}{7540}$ S

6661

Secret.   Crime Special

Instructions by I.V. from
Sinn Fein Head Quarters

County of Kerry

Caherciveen 14.. 5 .. 1918

I beg to State that I have received
information that instructions has been
issued by Sinn Fein Head Quarters
to the Irish Volunteer Organization,
that in all cases, where members are
in future arrested and tried for
political offences, drilling etc. & that
they are given the option of bail, in
all cases they are to enter into bail.

The object of this is to keep all
the members at home, pending conscription,
and not have the organization weakened
by the lodgement of its members in
Jail.

W. J. McLean Sgn 60 300

The D.I.   Caherciveen 14. 5. 18

Submitted. This appears consistent
with the action of Prisoners undergoing
sentence who have recently given bail.

The C.I.   R. Hicks

Sinn Fein meeting at Skibbereen

Co.Cork W.R.

Skibbereen, 31st March 1918

I beg to report that while on Patrol
on last night the 30th inst with Sergt
Malone a Sinn Fein meeting was
held on the Square, Skibbereen about
10.30 p.m. Addresses were delivered
by Peter O'Hourihane, Poundlick,
Michael Collins, Rosscarbery, Gerald
O'Sullivan a teacher in Carlow College +
James Duggan High St Skibbereen

Peter O'Hourihane addressed the meeting
on the subject of Bernie O'Driscoll's imprisonment + his going on hunger strike in
Cork Gaol. He was followed by Collins who
dwelt on the same theme, and referring to
the proceedings in Skibbereen Courthouse on
20th inst where J.B. O'Driscoll was charged
with using language inciting to the commission of Crime. M. Collins said "Bernie
"O'Driscoll was imprisoned for advising the
"Volunteers that if Ernest Blythe (who went on
"Hunger Strike in Cork Gaol) died in Gaol they
"the Volunteers) would take certain action
He declared

"If those words of Bernie O'Driscoll's means
"inciting to crime then I say in the presence
"of Police who are here making mental and
"other notes that I tender the very same advice
"that I stand where Bernie stood. That
"too is the advice I gave to the volunteers.
"Bernie cheered "up the Germans in the Courthouse
"You would think the Germans heard that
"cheer of Bernies for on the very same day
"they (the Germans) captured 15,000 British."

    Gerald O'Sullivan speaking on the same
subject said, after referring to the Police
as being their principal enemys & advising
no one to speak to them "The British threat-
"ened to torture the Commanders of German
"submarines they captured, but the Germans
"retorted that if they did, they the Germans
"would kill 5 British officers for every
"one of them they illtreated. This had the
"desired effect, and I now declare that
"if anything serious happens to Bernie O'Driscoll
(who is on hunger strike in Cork Gaol)
"then we too can make similar refusals
"and the volunteers here know when & how
"to do it." O'Hourihane & Duggan
spoke in a similar strain but were
cautious not to use any strongly prov-
ocative language

                    Josh McCarthy
                    Const 52,676

Sinn Fein meeting at Skibbereen on night of 30.3.18

County of Cork W.R.

Skibbereen 31.3.'18

I beg to report that I was present on duty at a Sinn Fein meeting which was held at the Square Skibbereen about 10.30pm on night of 30th inst The meeting was attended by about 80 Sinn Feiners who marched to the meeting place in four deep formation accompanied by a band. The meeting was addressed by Peter O'Hourihane Poundlick Skibbereen 40 years, Michael Collins Rosscarbery, Gerald O'Sullivan 27 years a teacher in Carlow College and a native of Coolnagrane Skibbereen and James Duggan 40 years High Street Skibbereen. Peter O'Hourihane spoke to the gathering on the Square and referred to the treatment of Barney O'Driscoll in Cork gaol. and the principles he was fighting for. O'Hourihane then introduced Michael Collins, as Mihaul Cullane (Irish) to the meeting. The latter also referred to the treatment of Barney O'Driscoll in Cork gaol and the charge on which he was arrested and imprisoned that of inciting to crime. He, Collins said that the words of advice Barney O'Driscoll gave them when he spoke here on this spot were the words of advice he would also give them and probably the police will be taking The H.C. Const.

mental notes and other notes of what is being said here to night and if they want to know if I am inciting to crime I say "I am" and if anything happens Barney O'Driscoll I hope every Irish Volunteer will know what to do.

Peter O'Hourihane next introduced Gerald Sullivan to the meeting and the latter addressed the gathering and referred to the treatment of Barney O'Driscoll in Cork gaol. He said that when The British Government notified their intention of taking reprisals for the sinking of ships and their crews by German Submarine Commanders in the present war the Germans replied to them and told them that for every German killed by them they would shoot five British officers and now, we, The Irish Volunteers can send the British Government the same message and I hope that every Irish Volunteer will stand by Bernie O'Driscoll whether he is now dead or alive. The next speaker was James Duggan High Street Skibbereen. His address was short and on the same subject as previous speakers. After the meeting the Sinn Feiners who attended the meeting marched through the streets of the town of Skibbereen accompanied by the Baltimore band and afterwards dispersed. Apart from cheering and an occasional shout of "Up Dublin" there was no disorder at the meeting

Patrick J. Malone
Ser 59050

SECRET.

County Inspector's Office,

Longford 11 May 19 18

Submitted: This man Collins is spending a lot of time at Granard in company with the local Suspects.

To C.I.

Reginald Heard
C.I.

Detective Office
Dublin 31/5/18.

Beg to report that Suspect Michael Collins was picked up here on 10th inst. but Suspect P.D. Cusack was not picked up or traced in the city about that time

The Supt. S. Dunn

Geo. Love.
Inspr

The Chief Comm.
Submitted
Owen Brien
Supt. 31/5/18

County of Cork. W.R.

B. Special

District of Skibbereen

Summary re Persons who existed to oppress at Skibbereen on 30. 3. 18.

No.	Name etc. of offenders	Address	Principal overt acts to be proved against each.	Names of witnesses
1	Michael Collins about 30 yrs. of age. Farmed a farmer's son, now a clerk. I am informed.	Cork City (named whom he stores plain his stores due)	Advised that the Irish Volunteers meant to oppress in case Mr. B. O'Donnell suffers from "hunger strike" in Gaol, and as the Germans threatens an Britain & were threa.	Head Cons. J. Hennessy Sergt. P.J. Walsh Const. Const. A. Carter D. J. Foster
2	Gerald O'Sullivan about 26 yrs. of age. Teacher in College.	Carlow (near town), now on a holiday at Skibbereen	Ditto	Ditto

Skibbereen 1. Apl. 1918

[signature]

The County Inspr.

5959

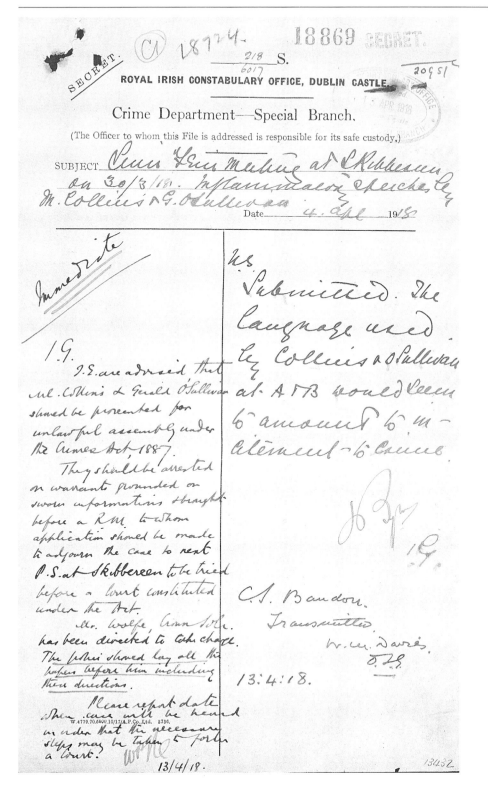

SECRET.   18869   SECRET.

CA 18724
218/6017 S.
20951

ROYAL IRISH CONSTABULARY OFFICE, DUBLIN CASTLE.

Crime Department—Special Branch.

(The Officer to whom this File is addressed is responsible for its safe custody.)

SUBJECT *Sinn Fein meeting at Skibbereen on 30/3/18. Inflammatory speeches by M. Collins & G. O'Sullivan*

Date _____ 4. Apl 19 18

Immediate

I.G.

I.S. are advised that Mr. Collins & Gerald O'Sullivan should be prosecuted for unlawful assembly under the Crimes Act, 1887.

They should be arrested on warrants grounded on sworn informations & brought before a R.M. to whom application should be made to adjourn the case to next P.S. at Skibbereen to be tried before a court constituted under the Act.

Mr. Wolfe, Crown Soln. has been directed to take charge. The police should lay all the papers before him including these directions.

Please report date when case will be heard in order that the necessary steps may be taken to form a court.

W.4779.70.6000.10/17/A.P.Co.,Ltd. 5736.

13/4/18.

U.S.

Submitted. The language used by Collins & O'Sullivan at A & B would seem to amount to an element to cause.

I.G.

C.I. Bandon.
Transmitted.
W.M. Davies
D.I.

13.4.18.

13432

3500,Wt.4617,1.08,H.Ltd.

64637c

Form $\frac{38}{F.R.}$

20615
Noted

ROYAL IRISH CONSTABULARY.

County of _Longford_

District of _Granard_.   Sub-District of _Ballinamuck_.

OUTRAGE.

*State the nature of the Outrage, and on whose person or property, &c.

Further Report of *_Inciting to Raid for Arms._
The Public.

1. Date of Original Report, and by whom reported to Head Quarters.   _4 : 4 : 18._ _S. I. Collins_

3. Persons made amenable since last Report, stating names, ages, and class in life, and whether by arrest or otherwise, giving dates.   —

2. Dates of further Reports, exclusive of this.   —

NOTE.—When a case is returned for Trial, it should be stated whether at Quarter Sessions or Assizes.

Dated at _Granard_ this _4th_ day of _July_ 19_18_.

STATEMENT.

With reference to my Report of the

4th April last, I beg to
report that on 28th ult. the
Crown obtained an order in
the High Court of Justice
removing the above case to
the next Assizes to be
held in the City of Londonderry.
It is not yet known when
the Assizes will be held.
Please _see file_ $\frac{64637}{20615}$ c. 31 : 5 : 18.

Chas. Collins
2D.T.

The Inspector General.

64637
27279
2065

Royal Irish Constabulary.

King V. Michael Collins.

Forfeiture of Recognizances.

COUNTY OF LONGFORD

GRANARD 5th Oct. 1918.

I beg to report that Michael Collins was arrested in Dublin on 2nd April 1918 on a charge of inciting to crime in a speech made at a Sinn Fein meeting at Legga, Ballinamuck on 31st March last. On the day following his arrest he was brought before the R.M. at Longford and returned for trial to next Assizes. He refused to recognize the court and was removed to Sligo Gaol, but on 22nd April he was released on bail, his sureties being two Longford shopkeepers.

On 28th June an order for change of venue to the City of Londonderry was granted, and on 17th July the defendant was called at Londonderry Assizes and failed to appear.

His last known address is 44 Mountjoy Street, Dublin, but his present whereabouts are unknown.

Notices relative to change of venue

were served on defendants' sureties and
left at his last known residence.
The prosecution was ordered on file
19373 C. 11: 3: 18.

Chas Collins
D.I.

Royal Irish Constabulary,
COUNTY OF LONGFORD.

County Inspector's Office,
LONGFORD 7 OCT 19 18

Submitted for Law Officers opinion
& direction — the Crown Sol' here. asks
for instructions as to whether he should
serve Notices on the Sureties in this
case to have the amount of recognizances
The accused Michael Collins did not
put any appearance at derry assizes
File 19373 C 11- 3. 18

Reginald Heard
C I

The Inspr General

County Inspector's Office,
Longford 15: 10: 18.

For your information.

Reginald Heard

D/Granard.

County Inspector,
R. I. Constabulary.

(3459.) Wt. 6369—550. 2000. 12/17. A.T.&Co.,Ltd.
(1417.) Wt. 1644—021. 2000. 5/18.

No. 26671/18

Chief Secretary's Office, Ireland.

JUDICIAL DIVISION.

SUBJECT.	MINUTE.

SUBJECT.

W. Longford

Rex v Mel. Collins
Inciting to crime.

Accused who was on bail
failed to appear to take his
trial at Londonderry Assizes
on 17th July 1918 whereupon
on the application of the Crown
the judge forfeited the recognizances
and ordered a Bench
warrant to issue for the
arrest of the accused.

The Crown Solicitor,
Mr Delany, now enquires 2/10/18
through the police if he
is to carry out the directions
of the Court and levy
the amount of the
recognizances —

DESP'D. & REG'D.
12 OCT. 1918

MINUTE.

Thro Dr Coyne
Attorney General
Please
advise W.W.M.

9. 10. 18.

Attorney General
Please advise. If the
judge made the usual order
I can see no reason why
the proper notices should
not be served & the usual
application made W.W.W.
10-10-18

I agree
A.W.S.
10, 10, 18

Under Secretary
Please see attorney General's
advice W.W.W. 10-10-18
I so informed Mr Delany Co
I I
II Inform Ly.
done 12/10   11. 10 18

Immediate   C. S

Impending meetings to demand
Release of political prisoners

            County of Cork W R
Clonakilty 2· 1·1919
    I beg to submit annexed
newspaper cutting from which
it would appear M. J. Collins
M P for this Division is to be
here and address a meeting
in Clonakilty on Sunday
next. This young man has
been "on the run" since the
arrests and internments
by the present Government of
a considerable number of persons
some 9 months ago. I understand
there is besides a Bench warrant
in existence for him as having
failed to answer to his recognizance
at the Derry Winter or other assizes
The Co Inspr Bandon   in

in 1918. I beg to apply
for instructions as to
whether he should now
be arrested if he appears
here. If so I should call
in the local military to
assist. I also beg to ask
if the proposed meeting
should be allowed. the fact
of Cork w being a special
military area may render
the holding of such a meeting
particularly objectionable
for it will inevitably draw
many objectionable and
unauthorised persons into
the town and area. I
am sending a copy of this
report to the Commandant
at Bandon.

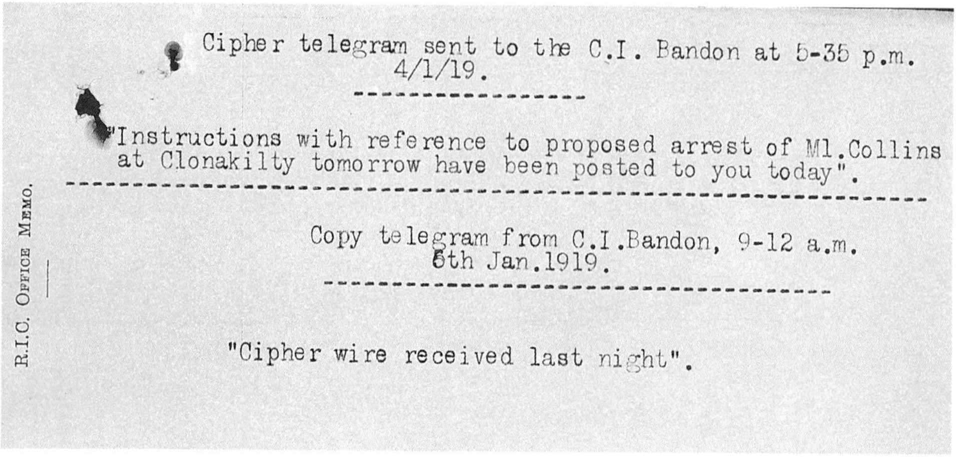

R.I.C. OFFICE MEMO.

Cipher telegram sent to the C.I. Bandon at 5-35 p.m. 4/1/19.

"Instructions with reference to proposed arrest of Ml.Collins at Clonakilty tomorrow have been posted to you today".

Copy telegram from C.I.Bandon, 9-12 a.m. 5th Jan.1919.

"Cipher wire received last night".

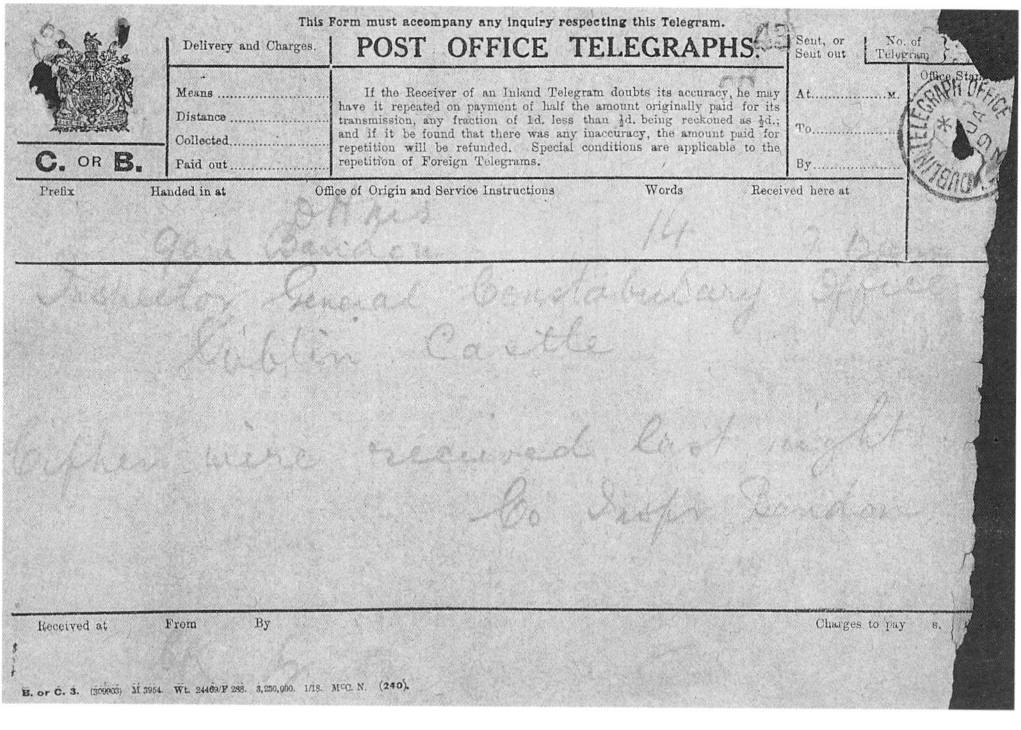

This Form must accompany any inquiry respecting this Telegram.

POST OFFICE TELEGRAPHS.

C. OR B.

Delivery and Charges. Means ... Distance ... Collected ... Paid out ...

If the Receiver of an Inland Telegram doubts its accuracy, he may have it repeated on payment of half the amount originally paid for its transmission, any fraction of 1d. less than ½d. being reckoned as ½d.; and if it be found that there was any inaccuracy, the amount paid for repetition will be refunded. Special conditions are applicable to the repetition of Foreign Telegrams.

Sent, or Sent out ... At ... M. To ... By ... No. of Telegram

Office Stamp: DUBLIN TELEGRAPH OFFICE

Prefix	Handed in at	Office of Origin and Service Instructions	Words	Received here at
	9am Bandon	DHQrs	14	9 Ba[...]

Inspector General Constabulary Office
Dublin Castle

Cipher wire received last night
Co Inspr Bandon

Received at ... From ... By ... Charges to pay ... s.

B. or C. 3. (309903) M 3954. Wt. 24469/F 288. 3,250,000. 1/18. McC. N. (240).

SECRET.

218 S.
13596

ROYAL IRISH CONSTABULARY OFFICE, DUBLIN CASTLE.

Crime Department—Special Branch,

(The Officer to whom this File is addressed is responsible for its safe custody.)

SUBJECT _Suspect Michael Collins_

Date 4. _Jany_ 19 19

Bandon 6.1.19
For your information
& compliance,
please

M Greer.

1 D.I. for C.I.
notallocated

D.I. Clonakilty

W.4779.70.5000.10/17/A.P.Co.,Ltd. 3736.

C.I. Bandon

East minutes of this date is
sent for your guidance.
The Bench warrant
is apparently in the
hands of the D.I. at
Derry with whom
you will have to
apply for it.
As Collins is ex-
pected at Clonakilty
tomorrow, the R.M.
should be consulted
& if he consents to
issue a warrant
on sworn information
for the arrest of this
man pending the
arrival of the Bench
W.T, the arrest should
be made, bearing

in mind the directions
of govt as to time & method.

J.E. Holmes

for I.G.

P.S. Please report tomorrow
what action has been taken

Clonakilty 6 : 1 : 1919

I beg to report in conformity with
instructions

32710

Royal Irish Constabulary Office.

DUBLIN CASTLE.

2 APR 1919

Administrative Division.

SUBJECT.	MINUTE.

SUBJECT.

Cork W.R.

Mr. Collins M.P.
Clonakilty 31.III.19
I beg to state the
description of Micl
Callins M.P. is as
follows vzg—

Clean shaven youthful
appearance and
dresses well Generally
wears trilby hat and
fawn over-coat
Dark Brown eyes
regular nose fresh
Complexion
medium actual make
oval face dark
hair 5ft 11 inches
high and 30 years
of age

J. M. Lowden

The
Bandon

(3824.) Wt.192—95.10,000/4) 15.A.T.&Co.,Ltd.

MINUTE.

D.I. Clonakilty

Please furnish a
description of Michael
Collins M.P. who is said
to be a native of Clonakilty
& who is wanted for an
offence of illegal drilling
in the Skibbereen district
& for failing to appear
to take his trial at
Londonderry Assizes on the
charge of inciting to raid
for arms in Co. Longford

W. M. Dewis

S.I.
28/3/19

16828

Secret & Immediate $\frac{218}{1359}$ 0   Crime Special

22524

Impending meetings to demand
release of political prisoners.

Cork W.R.
Bandon 3/1/19

N.S.   Submitted for instructions as
Submitted to whether Michael Collins, M.P.,
it is pre- should be arrested if he attends
sumed that the Clonakilty meeting on 3rd
the internment instant
order against   Previous papers dealing with
Mr Collins Collins are $\frac{218}{6017}$ s. 4/4/18 & $\overline{20951}$ C
should not 13/4/18 & 2/7/18
be executed,
but there is also   Mr Greer
a bench warrant
for his arrest issued
by the judge at Derry   1 D.I. for C.I
City Assizes of the   not allocated
July 17 last, vide Insp. General
file 64637 C
attached
I request the favour of
early instructions today as
to whether he w⁰ should be
executed if Collins turns up at
Clonakilty tomorrow. He is an
important suspect. He is adjt. genl. of the
Irish Volunteers & now M.P. for S. Cork

K
6544   4/1/19

Suspect Michl J. Collins
M.P. for South Cork and
adjutant General Irish Volunteers

County of Cork W.R.

Clonakilty 6 January 1919

I beg to ack receipt of annexed
file and instructions thereon
which I have read and copied.
The suspect in question did
not turn up in Clonakilty
yesterday. The meeting which
he proposed to hold and
address here having been
prohibited by the Commandant
of the Military area of Cork
W.R. and the prohibition
having been promulgated on
evening of Saturday 4th inst
by written notices and verbal
warnings to promoters the
idea of holding it was dropped
and

[left margin annotations:]

N.S.
Submitted
Mr Collins
did not go
to Clonakilty
the meeting
there having
been pro-
hibited by
the C.M.A., &
he was not
arrested.

7/1/19   19
Under Secretary
was submitted
WMC 8/1/19

The Inspector General

Collins was evidently advised
of the prohibition of his meeting
did not come to Clonakilty
at all. He however turned
up at Dunmanway instead
The probability of his endeavouring
to hold in Dunmanway the
meeting prohibited in clonakilty
was foreseen by police of the
latter town early and duly
ciphered to me. Later in the
day our scouting parties here
discerned a movement of leaders
of the Sinn Fein Party by indirect
routes towards Dunmanway.
In view of these facts I despatched
a Hd Const with one Const and
7 soldiers towards the latter
town. On their arrival there
was a meeting in progress
which Collins had addressed
but on hearing of the approach
of the police and military bolted
and disappeared through fields
and by-ways. He evidently
expected

he would be arrested and
that the composite military
and police party were
going (or coming) to arrest
him. He has evidently
fled and is not about
here. However I have
ciphered to Derby requesting
the warrant be forwarded
to me that he may turn
up again. The meeting
Collins was addressing at
Dunmanway consisted largely
of the R.I.C. Congregation.
It was stopped (after his
departure) by police and
military as being the same
meeting prohibited at
Donakilty. the days preceding

will be fully reported
without delay and
consulting upon this evening
as directed

22524

Under Secretary

Submitted for
orders with reference to
D.G.'s minute overleaf

WRL
4/
/

J.G.

It is not proposed at present
to arrest persons merely for internment
and the warrant in that regard may be
taken as temporarily suspended.

There is no discretion open to the
Govt. as regards the fourth warrant, & it
must be acted on. But of course care
will be taken to execute it in the manner
least calculated to cause public disturbance
or excitement, & if it is essential that the
warrant shd. be in the hands of the offcr.
who makes the arrest that point shd. be
seen to.

MWM
2/1

Judge ordered the forfeiture of his recognizances.
Please see file 64637/20615 b. 21: 5: 18.

Chas. Collins.
2.D.?

To C.I. Longford
for report

[signature]
D.I.
7/3/19

1. Ask C.I. what steps
have been taken to have
the warrant against
Collins executed.

2. To Under Sec.

W. [signature]
D.I.
10/3/19

IMMEDIATE.

COUNTY INSPECTORS OFFICE, R.I.C.
Date 8 MAR 19
LONGFORD.

I beg to state that Collins
has not been here since and is
not likely to come here — He
lives in Dublin — I see by
today's paper he met Gunnell
Cosgrove & others returning at
Kingstown pier accompanied by
Harry Boland on yesterday.

Done
10/3.

I.G.

The report called for
is awaited. Have the D.M.P.
been communicated with &
what is their view as to
possibility of arresting
Collins?

[signature]
The C.G.

Reginald Heard
C.I

To C.C. D.M.P.
W. [signature]
11/3/19

W.R.H.
10/3/19
D.I.

No. 2517

Tele: "DAMP, DUBLIN."   DUBLIN   METROPOLITAN   POLICE. 2 MAR 1919
No. 22.

CHIEF SECRETARY'S
Detective Department,
6778 - 13 MAR 1919
Dublin, 12th March, 1919.
OFFICE

Subject........................... MICHAEL COLLINS, M. P. ....

With reference to attached I beg to report
that Michael Collins has not resided at 44,
Mountjoy Street, Dublin, since his arrest on 2nd
April, 1918, and his present address is unknown.

He did not come under notice until about
three months ago since when he has publicly made
his appearance a few times in Dublin and the
country.

He has been observed here on a few occasions recently and was seen on morning of 10th
inst. when meeting some of the released intern-
ees at Westland Row Station.

W. McFeely,
Inspector.

The Under Secretary

If this man is located
here he can be
arrested - but he
apparently moves about
a good deal between
Dublin & the Provinces.

WE/Shustine
CC 17/3/19

The Superintendent,
Detective Dept.

19. The report
called for on the
10th is awaited.
WEK.
13/3/19.

The Chief Commr
Submitted.
Owen O'Brien
Supt 12/3/19

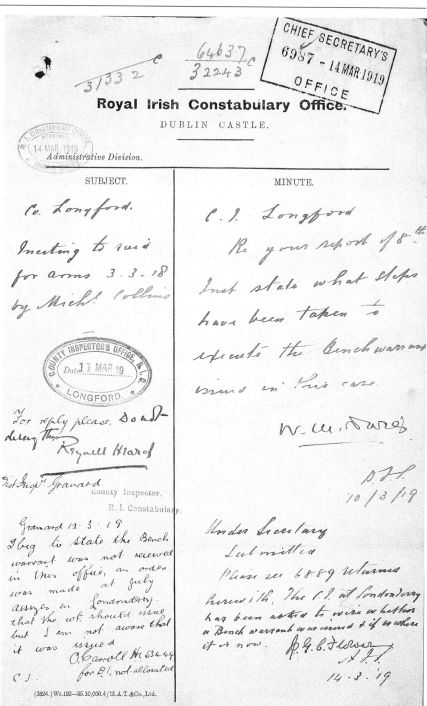

3133² c   64637 c   32243 c

CHIEF SECRETARY'S
6987 – 14 MAR 1919
OFFICE

Royal Irish Constabulary Office.

DUBLIN CASTLE.

R.I. CONSTABULARY OFFICE
RECEIVED
14 MAR 1919

Administrative Division.

SUBJECT.	MINUTE.

SUBJECT.

Co. Longford.

Inciting to raid
for arms 3. 3. 18
by Michl. Collins

COUNTY INSPECTOR'S OFFICE, R.I.C.
Dated 11 MAR 19
LONGFORD.

For reply please. So addressing the

Reginald Heard

Dist Supt Granard

County Inspector,
R. I. Constabulary.

Granard 12. 3. 19
I beg to state the Bench
warrant was not received
in this office, an order
was made at July
assizes in Londonderry.
that the wt. should issue
but I am not aware that
it was issued
O. Carroll No 53444
for 21 not allocated
C.J.

(3824.) Wt. 192—95.10,000.4/15. A.T. &Co., Ltd.

MINUTE.

C. I. Longford
Re your report of 8th.
Inst state what steps
have been taken to
execute the Bench warrant
sued in this case.

W. M. Davey

D.I.S.
10 / 3 / 19

Under Secretary
Submitted
Please see 6889 returned
herewith. The C. I. at Londonderry
has been asked to voice whether
a Bench warrant was issued & if so where
it is now.

A. G. C. Flower
A.I.

14 . 3 . 19

32283

Royal Irish Constabulary Office.

DUBLIN CASTLE.

Administrative Division.

SUBJECT.	MINUTE.
Co. Longford. Inciting to raid for arms by Michael Collins.	Under Secretary submitted with reference to papers sent to you on 11th Inst.
Decipher of telegram from C.I. at Londonderry :— Judge did not order issue of a Bench Warrant for arrest of Collins.	It would appear that Mc Collins is in Dublin. Please see attached cutting from "Evening Herald"

J.S.C. Glover

N.J.C.
15/3/19

6787 c c 5 $\frac{c}{3}$

18 MAR 1919
DUBLIN CASTLE

Chief Crown Solicitor
In connexion with file referred to you on yesterday. W.S.H.
15/3/19

Cutting from attached to
32242
J.P.
27/3/19

Evening Herald 14.3.-19.

(3824.) Wt.192—95,10,000.4/15.A.T.&Co.,Ltd.

Solicitor General

From this it appears that Collins
is probably in Dublin at present
I wrote after speaking to you
Saturday to Mr Delany C.S. to
prepare & swear affidavit &
apply for an adjournment
If the Cork warrant were
backed to the D.M.P. this
man might perhaps be arrested
today & if he were taken to
Cork tonight could be brought
before a magistrate there tomorrow
& remanded. But probably
it would be better just to
let an adjournt at Derry to next
assizes. I asked Mr Delany to have
the application for adjournt made
at the first possible moment so
that if Collins appeared the
Crown could ask the judge to put
him back or remand him on bail
for a day to enable wires to be sent
& have the Crown Solicitor & Crown witnesses
in attendance   JJ Mc 18-3-19

The Crown Solicitor witnesses should
be in attendance if prisoner.
does not appear a bench warrant
should be applied for to our
adjourned   JJ Mc
18/3/19

7097/19
32283

R.I. CONST... OFFICE
25 MAR 1919
DUBLIN CASTLE

Under Secretary

I have been informed the
Crown Solicitor who will attend
at Derry
I return the other files — having
detached Rent on Delany
the brief
The warrant for arrested
should be backed for execution
by the D.M.P. & defendant
arrested but it would be
well to defer executing the
warrant until after the Derry
assizes which open on 20th inst
as it is possible though not
likely that the defendant
may appear there.
It is also probable that the
judge in Derry will grant
a bench warrant

JJ Mc
18-3-19

Resubmit on 21/3/19 after Derry assizes.

19. The warrant on file
should now be backed for execution
in the D.M.P. area. A bench
warrant has been issued at the
Derry assizes   WM
22.3.19

Form No. 15,

BENCH WARRANT AT ASSIZES.

By the Lords Justices of Assize for the _North West_ Circuit.

COUNTY OF *the City of* Londonderry TO WIT. } WHEREAS, at a General Assizes and General Gaol Delivery, held at _Londonderry_ in and for the County of *City of Londonderry* on the _14th_ day of _July_ 1918, a Bill of Indictment was duly found against one _Michael Collins_ for that *he on 5º March 1918 unlawfully incited to Riot*

2º That he unlawfully incited to raid for arms

3º That he unlawfully incited to forcible Entry

4th That he unlawfully incited to assault on persons within the jurisdiction

5th That he unlawfully incited to steal arms

And the trial of the said Michael Collins having been adjourned to these present assizes on the 20th day of March 1919

and the said _Michael Collins_

has not appeared to abide his trial on the said Indictment. These are therefore in Her Majesty's name to authorize and strictly charge and command you and every of you, immediately on sight or on receipt hereof, to apprehend the Body of the said _Michael Collins_

wheresoever he may be found within the said County, and him so apprehended forthwith in safe custody to convey before one of Her Majesty's Justices of the Peace for the said County, that he may be further dealt with according to law. And for your and every or any of your so doing this shall be your sufficient Warrant.

Dated this _20th_ day of _March_ 1919.

By the Court, _W Kenny_ _Judge of Assize_

Alfred Moore Munro {Clerk of the Crown and Peace for the said County.

To all Sheriffs, Peace Officers, and Constables within and throughout the said County and their respective Assistants.

64637   C 31. 5. 18   Form 38 F.R.
20615

noted.

ROYAL IRISH CONSTABULARY.

County of _Longford_

District of _Granard_   Sub-District of _Ballinamuck_

OUTRAGE.

* State the nature of the Outrage, and on whose person or property, &c.

Further Report of * _Inciting to raid for arms the Public_

1. Date of original Report, and by whom reported to Head Quarters.   4. 4. 18.   D.I. Collins

2. Date of further Reports, exclusive of this.   4. 7. 18   19. 7. 18   11. 2. 19

3. Persons made amenable since last Report, stating names, ages, and class in life, and whether by arrest or otherwise, giving dates.

NOTE.—When a case is returned for Trial, it should be stated whether at Quarter Sessions or Assizes. In cases where there is an acquittal the reason if known should be stated. When claims for compensation are heard, it should be stated, if known, whether there will be an appeal.

Dated at _Granard_ this 25th day of _March_ 1919

STATEMENT.

With reference to my Report of the 11th February. 1919.

I beg to report that the case against Michael Collins was again for hearing at last Londonderry assizes he did not appear & a fresh Bench warrant was issued for his arrest.

P. Carroll Hd. Constable

for D.I. not allocated

The I.G.

County Inspector's Office.
R.I.C. LONDONDERRY.
31st day of March 1919

For report please
Derry   C. Clery CI

C.I. Londonderry,
Please see report by Hd Const Carroll in opposite & ascertain whether a Bench warrant was really issued at the last Londonderry assizes against Michl Collins M.P. & if so in whose hands is it now?

W.M. Davies
S.I.G.

28.3.19.

Londonderry 31.3.'19

I beg to report that a Bench Warrant
has been issued and is now in my
hands. There was no previous Bench W.

         J. P. Ryan
         [?]

Co. Insp.

       County Inspector's Office,
       R.I.C. LONDONDERRY,
   1st day of April. 1919

Submitted.

       C. Clarry C.I.

The
Inspector General.

64637 c

32710

Pend 3662

County Inspector's Office,
~~~~~~ 1.4. 19
Submitted

The Inspr General

County Inspector's Office
R.I.C. LONDONDERRY
5th day of April, 1919

For report, please

C. O'Carr
Derry 6:4:19

1. Insert desert in H & C.
2. C.I. Londonderry
   what steps have
   been taken to execute
   the bench warrant?

I beg to report that the police
here were in search of defendant
who was said to be in the
city. I communicated with
D.M.P. & D? .... &
.... as to issue
of Bench Wt

J F Ryan

1 Don't

A.S. Syarks
A.I.C.
2/4/19

County Inspector's Office.
R.I.C. LONDONDERRY.
7th day of April 1919

Submitted

C. O'Carr

The Inspector General.

Bench Warrant

v

Michael Collins

County of Londonderry

Londonderry 14. 4. 19.

I beg to submit attached Bench
warrant against above named
for endorsement to and execution by
the Dublin Metropolitan Police

Offender. — Michael Collins

Offence. — Inciting to Raid for Arms &c

County &c } County Longford.
Where Committed

Where Offender } 44 Montjoy Street in the
is to be found } City of Dublin

His description is as follows —
Clean shaven — Youthful appearance —
Dresses well — dark brown eyes,
regular nose, fresh complexion, oval
face, active make, 5 ft 11 in high —
About 30 years of age — Dark hair
Generally wears trilby hat. fawn overcoat.
Inspr General

His description appears in the Hue and
Cry under County Longford.

I received a communication from the
D1 at Granard that the present
address of Collins is 424 Mountjoy
Street Dublin.   This seems to
be in the Dist of D. Division.

Although the Offence — "Inciting to Raid"
for arms &c. was committed in Longford.
the Bench warrant is really issued for
his failing to appear at Londonderry City.
Spring Assizes — March 19 and take his
trial there on that charge.   The case was sent
to Londonderry City Assizes on change of
Venue.

     Please see file $\frac{64637}{32710}$ C. Vol. 19.

                              J. F. Regan
                                 D1.

(G. C). — Certificate

I certify that I have reason to believe that the person against against whom the within warrant was issued is to be found at 44 Mountjoy Street in the County of Dublin City and that I believe the signature to the within warrant to be in the handwriting of the said Justice

J. F. Ryan

Signed { To whom this warrant was delivered for execution

This 14 day of April 1919

To.
Inspector General
RIC
Dublin Castle.

(G. C) Certificate

It being certified to me as above, I here by in dorse the within warrant for execution in the said County of

Signed

Inspector General Royal Irish Constabulary
Dublin Castle

This   day of   19

32710

Warrant v Michael Collins

County of Londonderry

Londonderry 15. 4. 1919.

I beg to say that on 7. 7. 18.
I received an arrest warrant for
execution against above named.

It was issued at suit of Dist.
Inspector Foster of Skibbereen,
for Unlawful Assembly. It was
first endorsed to D.I. at Longford
for execution and subsequently
re-endorsed to me as Collins
was to appear at Derry City assizes
on change of Venue — Inciting to Raid
for Arms — from Longford.
He did not appear. and the warrant
                    unexecuted.
was returned to the County Inspr.
here on 19. 7. 18 attached to files
6637 ̸ C. 6. 7. 18 and 3148 ̸ 1. 7. 18
21272   8940

As I submitted a Bench warrant
for endorsement to D.M.P. against this
man on Yesterday, I think it right

C.I.

to bring under my authorities Notice
the issue of the warrant from the
Skibbereen District lest any confusion
might arise

     When submitting Bench warrant,
I quite forgot to refer to the other
warrant

     Collins is unknown to any police-
man here. I have not Communicated with
the Dist Inspro at Longford or Skibbereen in
the matter

            J F Ryan
            ID J

          County Inspector's Office
           R.I.C, LONDONDERRY.
          15th day of April 1919

     Submitted. I beg to say warrant was
returned to Ad Hrs 20. 7. 18

         J. F. Ryan
          C J.

          for Clonbars

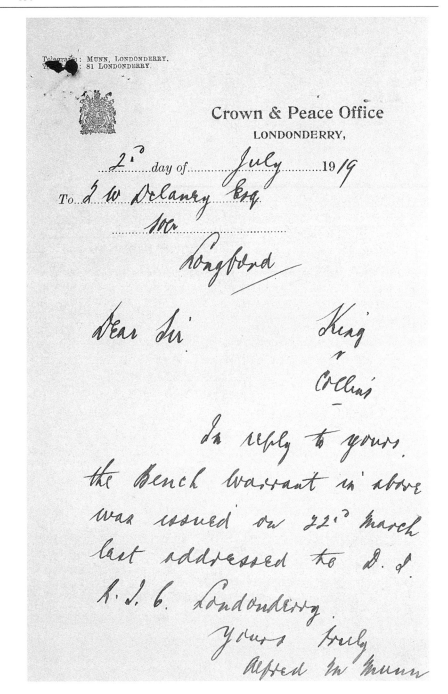

Telegrams: MUNN, LONDONDERRY.
81 LONDONDERRY.

Crown & Peace Office
LONDONDERRY,

2ᵈ day of July 1919

To ℒ W Delancy Esq.

10cr

Longford

Dear Sir   King
                             r
                           Collins
                            —

In reply to yours.
the Bench Warrant in above
was issued on 22ᵈ March
last addressed to D. J.
R. J. C. Londonderry.

Yours truly

Alfred M Munn

Encl.

T. W. DELANY,

SOLICITOR.

TELEGRAMS: DELANY. LONGFORD.
TELEPHONE Nº 14 LONGFORD.

Longford.

July 3rd   1919

Heard, Esq., C.I.,
                    Longford.

Dear Heard,   King V Collins

            I enclose letter from the
Clerk of the Crown and Peace. Please
say if the warrant has been executed.

            Faithfully yours,

                    JWDelany

32710

Execution of Bench Warrant.
King. V. Collins

4 JUL 1919

COUNTY OF LONGFORD

County Inspector's Office,
LONGFORD JUL 19 19

C. I. Longford
The warrant
has not yet
been executed.
All efforts to
trace Collins
have failed
for so far.

Y. Bennett
acting
ₚ.ₛ.
4. 7. 19

Submitted: I attach letter from the Crown
Solicitor. Longford asking whether the Bench
warrant issued at Londonderry Assizes on
22ᵈ March 19 V Michael Collins has
yet been Executed —
the warrant was issued by Judge Kenny and
addressed to D.I. RIC Londonderry whom
I understand forwarded it to H. qᵗˢ for
Execution by A. M. P. —
Please see 38 F.R. forwarded by D.I. Granard
25. 3 19 — also File 31332 C 10/3/19
regarding same matter.

Reginald Hsard
CI

Punctual

The Insp Genl
Longford
6ᵗʰ July 19
For your information. I have informed
the
D.I Granard

Crown Sol. Longford, accordingly

Reginald Heard

C1

Granard 7. 7. 19

Read & copied

P. Carroll H₂ 534646 /on D1

on leave

The C-1

County Inspector's Office, R.I.C.
Date 8 JUL 19
Longford

Read and Copied.

Reginald Heard

The Inspr Genl.

County Inspector,
R. I. Constabulary.

T. W. DELANY.
SOLICITOR.
TELEGRAMS: DELANY, LONGFORD.
TELEPHONE Nº 14, LONGFORD.

Longford.

July 12 1919

Dear Shaw

King v Collins

The Attorney
General has directed
"no further proceedings
need be taken"

J. J. Shaw

G Shaw for C I RIC

Longford

Dec 13.'19

King V. Michael Collins

Longford.
13. July 19

For your information

Resident Head
CI

D/ (handed.
14.7.19

Transmitted & circulated for
information   Read and copied
D Keeffe 207

HC & Supts.

CI

P.S I have informed my District
force and the Chief Commission
D.M. Police who I am informed
holds the warrant. + D1 London
derry..
D.K.D1

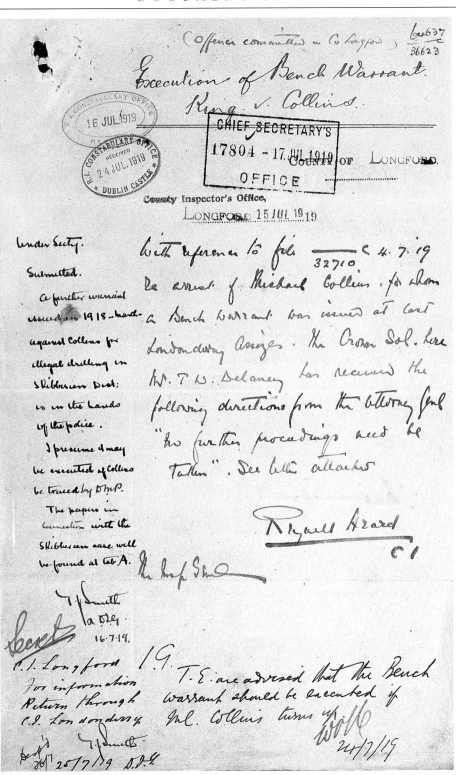

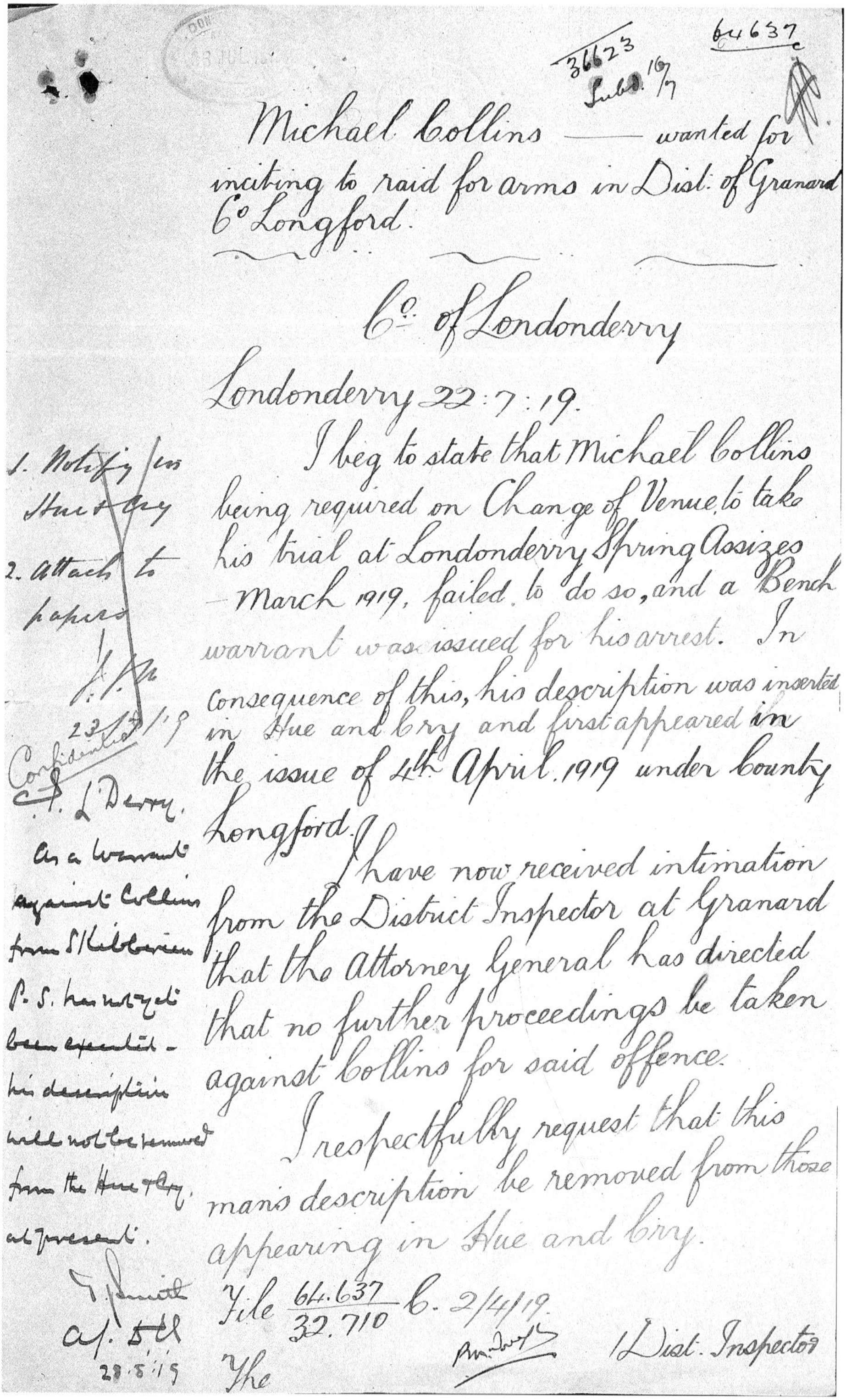

36623
Sub.⁹/₇

64637 c

Michael Collins —— wanted for inciting to raid for arms in Dist. of Granard Co Longford.

Co. of Londonderry

Londonderry 22 : 7 : 19.

I beg to state that Michael Collins being required on Change of Venue, to take his trial at Londonderry Spring Assizes — March 1919, failed to do so, and a Bench warrant was issued for his arrest. In consequence of this, his description was inserted in Hue and Cry and first appeared in the issue of 4th April 1919 under County Longford.

I have now received intimation from the District Inspector at Granard that the Attorney General has directed that no further proceedings be taken against Collins for said offence.

I respectfully request that this man's description be removed from those appearing in Hue and Cry.

File 64.637 / 32.710 C. 2/4/19.
Yke

1 Dist. Inspector

Left margin notes:

1. Notify Jess Start Cry

2. Attach to papers

J. M.
23/8/19
Confidential
C.I. L Derry.

As a warrant against Collins from S'Killbarien P.S. has not yet been executed - his description will not be removed from the Hue & Cry at present.

J. Smith
c.f. 5th
28.8.19

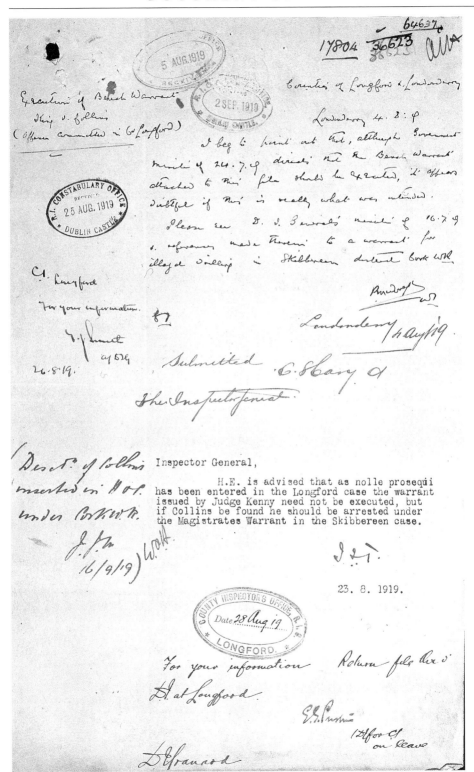

Inspector General,

　　　　H.E. is advised that as nolle prosequi
has been entered in the Longford case the warrant
issued by Judge Kenny need not be executed, but
if Collins be found he should be arrested under
the Magistrates Warrant in the Skibbereen case.

23. 8. 1919.

86623   b4637 C
          39499

Royal Irish Constabulary Office.

DUBLIN CASTLE.

Box.
C1.

Administrative Division.

SUBJECT.   *Confidential*   MINUTE.

Warrant against
Michl. Collins
for unlawful assembly
at Skibbereen on
30/3/18

D.I. Skibbereen

Please obtain a few
duplicate warrants against
Collins. Send one of them
up here prepared for
endorsement & execution
in the County of Dublin

You can prepare others
for endorsement & execution
in any likely places
which occur to you.
The warrant already
issued is being held
by D.M.P.

Skibbereen, 8.10.19
I beg to state that this order will be
complied with.
Mr. G.R. O'Connor R.M. who issued the
original warrant is now serving at
Waterford; and the D.I. Const. on whose
information the Wt. was issued is dead.
I shall have an information sworn
by another man & Wt. issued by
Mr. P.S. Brady R.M. Bantry, but
I do not expect to find him convenient
before 15th instant.
J. Forte D.I.
C.S.

Bandon 9/10/19
Submitted
H. Greer D.I.
for C.I. only sgd

I.G.

(3824.) Wt.192—95.10,000.4/15.A.T.&Co.,Ltd.

Cutting from Irish Independent of 18 8 19

PENDENT, MONDAY,

DAIL EIREANN LOAN

MR. M. COLLINS, M.P., IN SOUTH CORK

Explaining the Dail Eireann loan to his constituents in South Cork, Mr. M. Collins, M.P., in an address at Dunmanway to some thirty delegates, said their policy was not one of negation and destruction, but of hard work and insistent endeavour. "In our short existence," he went on, "we have succeeded in making the cause of Ireland known in places where formerly the very name of our country was hardly heard of. On the political sympathy so established we can lay the foundation of future business co-operation and intercourse.

"In the most important countries of the world there are now to be found Consuls, acting on behalf of Irish interests. An Dáil has voted £10,000 for this service. The acquisition of land by the people has been approved by An Dáil, and in a short time we shall put before the people a comprehensive scheme to secure this, as well as a proposition to finance the scheme."

He authorised the collection of subscriptions for the loan, and said he would prefer 250,000 subscriptions of £1 each than 25,000 of £10 each. Those who could not subscribe £1 at once could with 19 others pay in 1s. a week, which would purchase a certificate each week.

Those present subscribed £400, and gave an assurance that South Cork would do its part. Messrs. Gerold O'Sullivan, M.A., and J. B. O'Driscoll sent telegrams investing £50 each in the loan. Miss Brown, Union Hall, presided at the meeting.

$\frac{218}{2319}\frac{S}{S}$ Secret & Crime Special

25694 SECRET.

CONSTABULARY OFFICE — Received 22 AUG 1919 Dublin

Cutting from Irish Independent of 18th August 1919 re an alleged meeting at Dunmanway at which M Collins M.P. for South Cork addresses his constituents.

County of Cork W.R.

Dunmanway 19. 8. '19

With reference to attached cutting from Irish Independent of yesterday respecting a meeting held here and addressed by M Collins M.P. for South Cork, I beg to point out that the press report on subject is groundless.

It appears that one Denis O'Connell of Ireland St, Skibbereen arrived here on Friday 15th inst. and remained for the greater part of the day at the house of Daniel McCarthy, East Green, and left for home, by bicycle, on same evening.

There was no trace of Michael Collins M.P. here on 15th inst, but his brother John Collins of Woodfield, Clonakilty was observed here on that date. He came by car and left by a similar conveyance for home that evening.

Gerald O'Sullivan and J.B. O'Driscoll referred to in attached cutting at 'A' were I understand in Cork jail on 15th inst and could not have sent a telegram from here except by special permission of the Governor of that institution. There is no

The First Instr   trace

Margin note (left):

Under Secretary.

Submitted. There is not a particle of truth in attached cutting from the Irish Independent apparently.

Michael Collins has been on the run for months past. Gerald O'Sullivan and J.B. O'Driscoll were in Cork gaol on the date in question. Such newspaper reports are calculated to do harm.

[signature]

a. forty.
22:8:'19.

$\frac{K}{2113}$

hero of Miss Brown "Union hall". She
was not observed on 15th inst. the
date on which presumably the meeting
or alleged meeting, was held.

It is the opinion of the police here
that the report contained in attached
cutting was sent by Denis O'Connell
of Skibbereen, who is employed on the
Staff of the "Southern Star" Skibbereen,
in order to procure subscriptions
for the "Dail Eireann Loan," by showing
that the matter was receiving the
sympathy and support of the
people of Dunmanway.

Bernard Reilly H.C. 53610

Clonakilty 20 : 8 : 19

Submitted   I can find
no trace of Mr. M. Collins M.P. having
visited this District and I believe the
newspaper report is incorrect. I caused the
house of John Collins of Woodfield, Clonakilty
to be searched early on the morning of the
19th inst., but Mr. Collins M.P. was not there.
No documents dealing with the Dail Eireann
Loan were found.

H.Connor. 2nd D.I.

The Co. Inspr.

Bandon 21 : 8 : 19
Submitted for information.
The Insp.l General   H.Connor 2DI. for CI.
                      on Inspn

Oáil éireann.

Seoltan Litpeaca cun Runaroe Dáil Eipeann, f/c Tige an Áro-Maoip, Át-Cliat.

Correspondence may be addressed to the Secretary, Dáil Éireann, c/o Mansion House, Dublin.

Mansion House,

DUBLIN.

30th December, 1919.

A Chara,

DAIL EIREANN LOAN.

Enclosed please find Prospectus and Application
Form of the above. May I hope that you will take an
early opportunity of showing your faith in the cause of
Ireland by taking an investment in the Government of
Ireland's Loan.

It is not necessary for me to emphasise the
importance of making this Loan of the Irish Republic
a success. The British Government – by its repressions,
by its activity against advocates of the Loan, by its
tyrannous attempts to suppress all reference to it –
has done that. Every supporter of the Irish Nation at
this hour has his or her duty clearly defined – it is to
support and help their own lawful Government against
the unlawful authority of the Foreigner.

Today our kindred in America are being asked to
lend 10,000,000 dollars. They are responding
magnificently, and their response will be still greater
when they see the people at home giving proof, by their
money, of their hope in the future of Ireland.

I enclose you in addition a copy of the letter
written by the venerable Archbishop of Dublin –
Dr. Walsh – the latest Ecclesiastical recommendation
of the Loan. The lead which the most eminent Divines
in Ireland are giving on the question will, I am sure,
be generously followed in South Cork.

        The South Cork Comhairle Ceanntair has divided
the Constituency into four parts and has placed a man
in charge of each.   In your district the man is
Mr. DENIS O'SHEA of CURRAGH, SKIBBEREEN.   I am asking
him to make arrangements to see that you are called on,
or perhaps you will kindly arrange to hand your
subscription to him or to some other member of the
Committee of the Skibbereen Cumann.   They will arrange
for transmission, and the official receipt will be sent
you as early as possible.   In the meantime, I would ask
you to let me know that this letter reaches you safely,
and to intimate what the amount of your subscription
will be.   You should not on any account send the money
through the Post to me.   It may, of course, be sent
to me by hand.

        At this time it is a matter of the greatest regret
to me that I am prevented from putting the position in
person before our supporters in South Cork.   You will
understand that the enemy anxiety to stop my activities
is so great that I cannot make the journey, even if I could
spare time from the duties which fall on me through
having to organise the Loan effort for all Ireland.

        With very best wishes for a happy New Year,

                              Do chara go buan,

                                   Mícéal O Coleaun

Encls.

1ASACT 1919—1 nÉ1R1nn

R1Aᵹ41CAS SAORSCÁ1C é1Re4nn.

b4nn4í cL4ꝃ1ᵹce (5%) Aꝓ £250,000 vá ᵹcuꝓ Aꝓ v1oL.

Co1ꝓꝓeoc4ꝓ 4n cuꝓ vꝓéꝓ 5 ꝼén ᵹcé4v ꝼ4 mbL14v41n ón L4 'n4 mbe1v n4 b4nn4í íocc4 1 n-1omL4n, 4c n1 v1oLꝼ4ꝓ 4n cuꝓ ꝼ4n 5o ce4nn ꝓé ꝓí c4ꝓé1ꝓ vo S4oꝓꝓc4c é1ꝓe4nn 4vꝓá1L e4v4ꝓná1ꝓ1únc4 vꝼáᵹ41L, 4ᵹuꝓ c4ꝓé1ꝓ voꝓ n4 S4ꝓ4n41ᵹ 1mce4cc 4ꝓ ꝼ4v 4ꝓ é1ꝓ1nn.

41S1OCꝼAR 4n 14ꝓ4cc 4ᵹuꝓ 5 ꝼén ᵹcé4v bꝓe1ꝓe 'n4 ce4nnc4 c4ov 1ꝓc1ᵹ ve ꝼíce bL14v41n c4ꝓé1ꝓ vo S4oꝓꝓc4c é1ꝓe4nn 4vꝓá1L e4v4ꝓná1ꝓ1únc4 vꝼáᵹ41L.

4n c-41ꝓᵹe4v 4 ᵹeobꝼ4ꝓ ve b4ꝓꝓ n4 h14ꝓ4cc4 ꝼo úꝓá1vꝼe4ꝓ é cun Cú1ꝓ n4 hé1ꝓe4nn 4 éꝓ4ob-ꝼc4o1Le4v von Vom4n móꝓ; cun bunu1ᵹce Conꝼul 1 ᵹCo1ᵹcꝓíoc41v vꝼonn Cꝓáccá1L n4 hé1ꝓe4nn vo ꝼé4vú; cun c4bꝓu1ᵹce Le Vé4ncúꝓ41v n4 hé1ꝓe4nn; 4ᵹuꝓ Le h-4ᵹ41v ꝓé O1bꝓe ná1ꝓ1únc4 4ꝓ 4 c1nnꝼív vá1L é1ꝓe4nn.

[ꝓóᵹꝓ4 ꝼe4ꝓ4 4ꝓ 4n vc4ob e:Le.

INTERNAL LOAN OF 1919.

GOVERNMENT OF THE IRISH REPUBLIC.

ISSUE OF

£250,000 5% REGISTERED CERTIFICATES.

Interest calculated at the rate of 5 per cent. per annum, from the date when the Certificates are fully paid, but not payable until a date Six Months after the Irish Republic has received International Recognition, and the English have evacuated Ireland.

REDEEMABLE at a Premium of 5 per cent. within Twenty Years of the International Recognition of the Irish Republic.

The proceeds of this Loan will be used for pro-pagating the Irish Case all over the World, for establishing in Foreign Countries Consular Services, to promote Irish Trade and Commerce, for fostering Irish industries, and, generally, for National Purposes as directed by Dáil Eireann.

[Prospectus Overleaf.

FÓGRA FEASA. (Le h-agaidh sintiús i nÉirinn).

Bannaí Cláruiġṫe (5%) ar £250,000 dá gcur ar díol.

Beidh ús le fáġail orṫa san ón lá 'na mbeid íocṫa i n-iomlán do réir 5 fén gcéad sa mbliadhain; agus íocfar an tús san gaċ leaṫḃliadhain—do réir na gcoinġeall atá sa ḃfógra feasa—ar an gcéad lá d'Eanair, agus ar an gcéad lá d'Iúl.

1. Tá úġdarás ó Dháil Éireann ag an Aireaċt na Bannaí sin roimhráidhte do díol leis an bpobul, agus glacfaidh an tAire Airgid iarratasaí 'na gcóir feasta.

2. Nuair imṫeoġaidh Arm Gall as Éirinn beidh an iasaċt so 'na ċéad éileaṁ ar Ṫeaċt isteaċ Saorstáit Éireann.

3. Díolfar na Bannaí ins na meadhonaiḃ seo .i. £1, £5, £10, £20, £50, agus £100; agus geoḃfar ús orṫa do réir £5 fén gcéad sa mbliadhain. Sé beidh sa gcéad ús a ġeoḃfar ná ús ón lá 'nar críoċnuiġeadh an íocaidheaċt, aċ ní ḃfaġfar san go ceann sé mí tar éis do Shaorstát Éireann admhail eadarnáisiúnta d'fáġail, agus tar éis dos na Sasanaiġ imṫeaċt as fad as Éirinn. Íocfar an tús 'na dhiaidh sin gaċ leaṫḃliadhain ar an gcéad lá d'Eanair agus ar an gcéad lá d'Iúl.

4. Sé luaċ an ċursa so ná £100 fén gcéad. Íocfar é ar an gcuma so:—

50 fén gcéad le linn iarratais.
25 fén gcéad an ċéad lá de Dheire Foġṁair.
25 fén gcéad an ċéad lá de ṁí na Nodlag.

5. Cuirtear iarratasaí ar Bannaiḃ maraon leis an íocaidheaċt le linn iarratais ċun an Aireaċ Airgid aon lá tar éis lá Luġnasa, 1919, i dtreo go dtaḃarfaí dos na hUrraiḃ iad

6. Taḃarfar admháil do gaċ iarratóir le linn íocaidheaċta dó, agus scríoḃfar ar an admháil sin méid na ceannuidheaċta agus an méid a h-íocadh le linn iarratais. Nuair a ḃeidh na Bannaí ullaṁ taḃarfar iad mar ṁalairt ar na h-admhálaiḃ sin.

7. Tá foirmeaċa clóḃuailte iarratais agus cóipeanna den ḃfógra feasa le fáġail ó Aire Airgid Dháil Éireann, ó Ċisteoiriḃ Oineaċa Sinn Féin, agus ó Rúnaidhe gaċ Cumainn de Ṡinn Féin i nÉirinn.

Éamonn de Valéra, Príoṁ-Aire.
Míċeál Ó Coileáin, Aire Airgid.

15adh lá Luġnasa.

PROSPECTUS. **(FOR HOME SUBSCRIPTION).**

ISSUE OF

£250,000 5% REGISTERED CERTIFICATES.

Bearing Interest from the date when fully paid, at the rate of 5 per cent. per annum, payable half-yearly on the 1st January and the 1st July, subject to the reservations contained in this Prospectus.

1. The Ministry of Dáil Eireann is authorised by An Dáil to issue the above Certificates to the public for subscription, and the Minister of Finance will receive applications until further notice.

2. After the withdrawal of the English Military Forces, this Loan becomes the first charge on the Revenues of the Irish Republic.

3. The Certificates will be issued in denominations of £1, £5, £10, £20, £50, and £100, and will bear interest at the rate of £5 per cent. per annum. The first dividend will consist of interest calculated from the date upon which the final payment is made, but will not be payable until a date Six Months after the Irish Republic has received International Recognition, and the English have evacuated Ireland. Thenceforward, payment will be made half-yearly on 1st January and 1st July.

4. The price of this issue is £100 per cent., payable at follows:—

50 per cent. on application.
25 per cent. on 1st October, 1919.
25 per cent. on 1st December, 1919.

5. Applications for Certificates, together with the amount payable on application, may be lodged on or after the 1st August, 1919, with the Minister of Finance, for deposit with the Trustees.

6. Every applicant will be supplied at the time of payment with a receipt, in which the amount of the purchase and the amount paid upon application will be recorded. The Registered Certificates will, when prepared, be issued in exchange for this receipt.

7. Printed Forms of Application and Copies of this Prospectus may be obtained from the Minister of Finance, Dáil Eireann; the Honorary Treasurers of Sinn Féin, and the Secretary of any Sinn Féin Club in Ireland.

EAMONN DE VALERA, President.
MICHAEL O COILEAIN Minister of Finance

15th August, 1919.

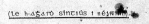

This form to be retained by local committee and forwarded to H. Q. with the amount paid.

No...............

FORM OF APPLICATION.   **1919 ISSUE (INTERNAL).**

Government of the Irish Republic.

ISSUE OF

£250,000 5% REGISTERED CERTIFICATES.

Issued at par, and bearing Interest at £5 per cent. per annum, payable half-yearly on the 1st January and 1st July, subject to the reservations contained in the Prospectus, but calculated from the date on which the final payment is made.

REDEEMABLE within Twenty Years of the International Recognition of the Irish Republic, at 105 per cent.

Date, ..., 1919.

To the Minister of Finance,

In terms of the Prospectus, dated 15th August, 1919, I/we hereby apply for .... pounds (£...........) of 5 p.c. Government of the Irish Republic Certificates, and tender herewith .... pounds (£...........) in payment, being Fifty Per Cent. (50%) of the amount applied for.*

And I/we agree to pay the balance due from me/us by the instalments specified in the Prospectus, and as set out hereunder—

25 per cent. on the 1st October, 1919.
25 per cent. on the 1st December, 1919.

.... Certificates of £1, £...........	.... Certificates of £20, £...........
.... Certificates of £5, £...........	.... Certificates of £50, £........... £...........
.... Certificates of £10, £...........	.... Certificates of £100, £...........

Ordinary Signature, ...

Name in full, ...
(State Mr., Mrs., Miss, or other title).

Address, ...

Occupation, ...

* Cheques, British P.O., and Drafts, should be crossed and made payable to the Trustees of Dáil Eireann.

Detach this part and return to Subscriber.

No...............

GOVERNMENT OF THE IRISH REPUBLIC.
5 per cent. Registered Certificates (1919) (Internal).

Date, ..., 1919.

RECEIVED from ....

of ....

the sum of .... pounds,... shillings, being

the amount payable on application for:—

MICHAEL O COILEAIN, Minister of Finance.

Per ....

£...................

Preserve this receipt carefully. It will be exchanged in due course for the definite certificate.

SECRET.

218 S.
22195

ROYAL IRISH CONSTABULARY OFFICE, DUBLIN CASTLE.

Crime Department—Special Branch.

(The Officer to whom this File is addressed is responsible for its safe custody.)

SUBJECT _Cutting from the Irish Independent of 18th inst. re alleged address by Mr. Collins at Dunmanway._

Date _26th August_ 19_19_

Bandon: 27. 8. 19

For very careful
enquiry.
Report fully re Miss
Browne.

Does John Collins
usually attend meetings
at a distance from C Iosakilty.
Has he any official position
in the Sinn Fein organisation
locally?

J Willbond
      6,

Co Iosakilty

C. Bandon.

Are the police quite sure that no such
meeting took place?

On 21st inst. the annual meeting of the Chief
Executive of Sinn Fein was held in Dublin
and Michael Collins, who is believed to have
been present, is reported in the press to have
referred to this meeting in Dunmanway the
previous Sunday stating that "£400 was
subscribed although there were only 25
persons present." He does not say he was
present but suggests that he was.
Is there such a person as Miss Brown of
Union Hall? If so, what is known of her.
Was she absent from her home on that date?

J S Collins

a folly

(6868).Wt.1197—77.5000.5/19. A.T.&Co.,Ltd.*

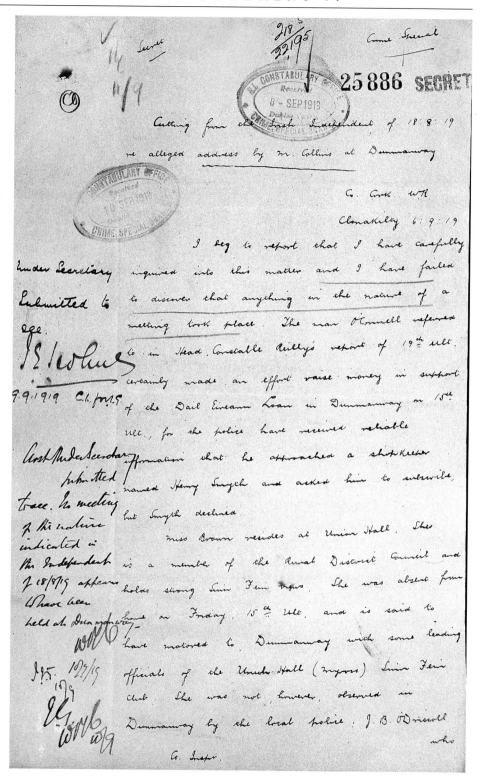

Secret   Crime Special

25886 SECRET

Cutting from the Irish Independent of 18·8·19

re alleged address by M. Collins at Dunmanway

C. Cork. W.R.

Clonakilty 6·9·19

I beg to report that I have carefully
inquired into this matter and I have failed
to discover that anything in the nature of a
meeting took place. The man O'Connell referred
to in Head Constable Reilly's report of 19ᵗʰ ult.
certainly made an effort raise money in support
of the Dail Eireann Loan in Dunmanway on 15ᵗʰ
ult., for the police have received reliable
information that he approached a shopkeeper
named Henry Smyth and asked him to subscribe,
but Smyth declined.

Miss Brown resides at Union Hall. She
is a member of the Rural District Council and
holds strong Sinn Fein views. She was absent from
home on Friday, 15ᵗʰ ult. and is said to
have motored to Dunmanway with some leading
officials of the Union Hall (Myross) Sinn Fein
club. She was not, however, observed in
Dunmanway by the local police. J. B. O'Driscoll
G. Inspr.   who

Under Secretary
Submitted to
see.

9.9.1919 C.I. for I.G

Asst Under Secretary
submitted
to see. No meeting
of the nature
indicated in
the Independent
of 18/8/19 appears
to have been
held at Dunmanway

who was arrested at Glandore on 13th ult. and
who is now in Cork Prison is a nephew of
miss Browns and it is suggested that she
may have motored to Cork on the 15th ult.
to see him

John Collins has been seen attending
meetings at a distance from Clonakilty, but
he occupies no official position in any local
S. F. organization.

I notice that mr Collins m.P. refers to a
meeting which was held on a Sunday. The
police are quite satisfied that no meeting
of the kind referred to was held in any
part of this District on a Sunday, and
miss Brown was not absent from her home
on any Sunday.

H Connor. 2nd D.I.

Bandon 8.9.19

Submitted

The I.G.   JWillord &

Crime Special

Secret

Dail Eireann Loan:

County of Cork WR.

Skibbereen 1: 1: 20:

I beg to state that annexed letter came into my possession today under circumstances of a very secret nature.

This document is signed by Michael Collins M.P. who is on the run, and seemingly at present staying in Dublin. According to this letter four men are appointed to deal with the Dail Eireann Loan in the Parliamentary Constituency of South Cork, and the three men whose names are not mentioned are believed to be acting at the centres of Dunmanway, Clonakilty, and Bandon.

As regards the Skibbereen District only a small area lies within the South Cork Constituency; and Michael O'Brien who is on the run was acting in the capacity the D.I.

of organizer for the Loan some time ago.

Denis O'Shea who is mentioned in the letter as collector for Skibbereen, is a well known local suspect, and was frequently searched within the past 6 months.

The O'Shea family are against this mans participation in Sinn Feinism, and recently information reached the police here that he had ceased to have any connection with the movement, and actually burned Sinn Fein literature he received. There may be a possibility that even though appointed O'Shea would not act. His movements and conduct are, however, under close supervision and steps will be taken at the most favourable moment.

— W. Mulheron Sergt 61,031.

Skibbereen, 1st Jan. 1920.
Submitted. This matter will be closely watched. I expect similar letters have been sent for circulation in other constituencies.

J. Foster

C.I.

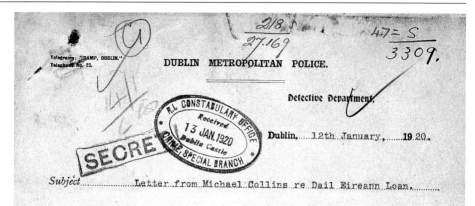

Telegrams: "DAMP, DUBLIN."
Telephone No. 22.

DUBLIN METROPOLITAN POLICE.

Detective Department.

R.I. CONSTABULARY OFFICE
Received
13 JAN. 1920
Dublin Castle
CRIME SPECIAL BRANCH

SECRET

Dublin, ...12th...January,......19.20..

Subject...............Letter..from..Michael..Collins..re..Dail..Eireann..Loan.............

To Insp. Sup.

Transmitted

Although the letter is
addressed from the Mansion
House Collins does not
either work there or frequent
it.
The matter of post letters
arriving there is dealt
with daily as at A.
There is nothing important
in any coming recently

W.C. Redmond
Ass Commr
12.1.20

A

I beg to report that no letters addressed to Michael Collins, Mansion House, have
been sent here from the G.P.O. although the
Lord Lieutenant's warrant authorises the
detention by the Post Office of all postal
packets transmitted by post to the Mansion
House, except those addressed to the Lord
Mayor or members of his family.

It has already been learned that com-
munications to Collins about the Loan ahould
be addressed to him and enclosed to certain
individuals in Dublin who could be relied
upon to make delivery.

It is most unlikely that Collins goes
to the Mansion House although the letter
purports to be addressed from there.

W.McFeely,
Inspector.

The Superintendent,
    Detective Dept.

The Chief Commr
Submitted.
Owen Brien
Supt. 12/1/20

R.I.C. Office Memo.

C.I. Cork & Bandon

Michael Collins believed to be in
South of Ireland probably Cork.
If located arrest him & lodge him
in Cork gaol under C.mas orders.

Ample force should be
assembled for arrest as seen
[...] here when arrested,

Done at 3½ Pm
5/12/19 P.M.S

218 S.
27/69

47⸗ S.
3309
D M P

Crime Special

Letter from Michael Collins M. P.
re the Dáil Eireann Loan.

County Clerk, C.C.R.

County Inspector's Office,

Bandon. 2. 1. 1920

Submitted. Apparently from this
Chief Commissioner. letter dated 20. 12. 19 Michael Collins
      Dup. M. P. is carrying on operations from the
To note. Mansion House Dublin. I am putting
all my S.I.O. on the alert re this
matter & taking steps to deal with
the men likely to be appointed to
further the Loan in the different
districts. It is clear Collins is
in communication with the Sinn Féin
organization in all counties in Ireland
in regard to the Loan

for Commr 3/1/20   The I. G

J Willard b.

ⓐ

918 S.
26213

ROYAL IRISH CONSTABULARY OFFICE, DUBLIN CASTLE.

Crime Department—Special Branch.

(The Officer to whom this File is addressed is responsible for its safe custody.)

SUBJECT *Michael Collins and Gerald O'Sullivan*

Date *2nd December* 1919

Supt C—

WL. J
a 6/12/19

Chief Commissioner, D.M.P.

Referring to the warrant held by
you for the arrest of Michael Collins
it appears from a letter recently seen
in the Provinces that this man is
stopping at the Clarence Hotel, Dublin.
On 25th ulto he is also said to have
paid a visit to 10 Mountjoy Square.
Gerald O'Sullivan, a released hunger
striker who should have returned to
prison on 28th ulto, has been seen in
Dublin with Collins.
A description of O'Sullivan, who should
be taken to Mountjoy if found, is
attached.

J.S. —————

a. J——

(6868).Wt.1197—77.5000.5/19.A.T.&Co.,Ltd.*

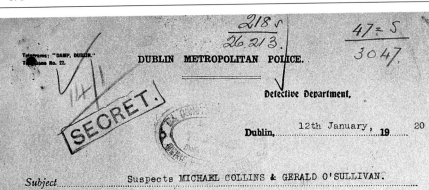

DUBLIN METROPOLITAN POLICE.

Telegrams: "DAMP, DUBLIN."
Telephone No. 22.

SECRET.

Detective Department,

Dublin, ...12th January, 19 20

Subject............Suspects MICHAEL COLLINS & GERALD O'SULLIVAN.

The Inspector General,

Transmitted.

Inquiries are being
continued. Collins uses
many postal addresses
W.C.F. Redmond
Ass Commr

                        With reference to attached files,
            I beg to report from inquiries I made I
            ascertained that Michael Collins is not
            staying at the Clarence Hotel nor can he
            be traced as having visited 10 Mountjoy
            Square on the 25th November, 1919.
                        Gerlad O'Sullivan is not lodging
            at 19 Cabra Road, neither is he staying at
            44 Mountjoy Street where he generally
            stops while in Dublin.
                        The particulars relating to each
            of the above suspects have been noted at
            the Special Branch of this Department and
            should they be located in this City they
            will be arrested.

                                    Denis O'Brien
                                        Det. Officer.

    The Supt., G. Divn.

                        The Chief Commr
                        Submitted.

                        Owen Breen
                        Supt 13/1/20

SECRET

218 S.
27.222

47 = S.
3434
D.M.P.

ROYAL IRISH CONSTABULARY OFFICE, DUBLIN CASTLE.

Crime Department—Special Branch.

(The Officer to whom this File is addressed is responsible for its safe custody.)

SUBJECT........ Michael Collins,

Wanted for Deportation.

Date........ 5/1/20. ....19......

C.I. Bandon,

With reference to
C. S. Circular of 19th ult. 94 1919.
information has been received
that the above-named (who is
wanted by the D.M.P.for
deportation) is at present at
Clonakilty or neighbourhood.

Bandon.   7. 1. 2 0.

*For immediate
inquiry. I have notified
D.I.s at Bandon &
Skibbereen*

*Willard
D.I.
C. Inokilty*

Clonakilty 8.1.20

*I beg to report that
Collins cannot be traced in this
District. Careful inquiry has been
made and and a number of
houses have been searched, but
without result. A close watch
will be kept and if Collins
is located I will have him
arrested.*

H Connor 1st S.I.

7750 c.i.

C.I.

for I.G.

Chief Commissioner Dublin.

*This inquiry was made in consequence of a
telephone message from Supt. Brien on
evening of 5th. In a recent letter Collins
declined to visit West Cork on the grounds
that it was too dangerous.*

(6868).Wt.1197—77.5000.5/19.A.T.&.Co.,Ltd.

Bandon 15:1:20
Submitted.
The D.I.s Bandon & Skibbereen
(adjoining Districts) report that
no trace of Collins has been
found in their Districts

There is reason to believe this man
is in Dublin still according to
local information in Skibbereen but his
address is not known.

The I.G.   Jno Mord By

Inspr Genl R.I.C.
Noted
     W. C. Redmund
       Ass Commr
       19:1:20

314 S.

28788

ROYAL IRISH CONSTABULARY OFFICE, DUBLIN CASTLE

S.

3927

SECRET

Crime Department—Special Branch.

(The Officer to whom this File is addressed is responsible for its safe custody.)

SUBJECT _Michael Collins_

Date. 8ᵗʰ March 1920

Supt G.

For necessary action.

DBarrett A.C.

9 : 3 : 20

Chief Commissioner Dms?

It is reported that the above-named is a constant visitor at the house of John P. Twohig, who is employed in the Irish Education Office. Twohig's house is Craigmellar, Haddon Road, Clontarf.

He also frequently visits Timothy Donovan 3 St. Michaels, Sarsfield Road, Inchicore.

These two men are uncles of Collins by marriage.

Collins has been observed walking about Dublin recently with Hannah O'Brien and Mary O'Brien who are employed at the G. P. O.

(6868).Wt.1197—77.5000.5/19.A.T.&.Co.,Ltd.*

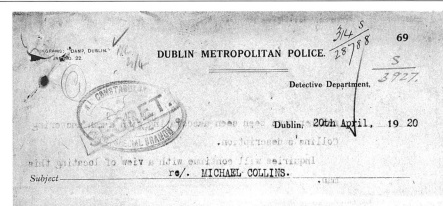

GRAMS: "DAMP, DUBLIN."
JNE NO. 22.

DUBLIN METROPOLITAN POLICE. 69

Detective Department,

Dublin, 20th April, 19 20

Subject _____ re/. MICHAEL COLLINS.

The Inspector General,

Transmitted.

D. Barrett.

Asst. Commissioner

20/4/20

With reference to attached I beg to state
that I have made every possible inquiry regarding the visits of Collins to the persons named,
but I am unable to ascertain if he calls there.

Twohig lives at the address given. He is
known to some of the Police at Clontarf and is
frequently seen by them going to and from business
He is a native of Co. Cork.

Timothy Donovan lives at the address given
and is employed at the Distillery, Chapelizod.
He is also a native of Co. Cork and is known
by some of the Police in Kilmainham. I cannot
ascertain if any of these men are uncles of
Collins as stated.

A Miss Hannah Brien and a Miss Nancy O'Brien
are the only persons of the name employed in the
G.P.O. Both are engaged in the Accounts Office,
Sackville Street and took the Oath of Allegiance
when requested to do so at the time all Civil
Servants were asked. There is a difference in
the names as the former is Brien and the latter
O'Brien. Miss Brien lodges at 40 De Courcy
Square with a Mr Straghan and Miss O'Brien lodges
at 89 Botanic Road. As far as I can ascertain
                                        neither

The Supt. G Division,

neither have been asscoiating with a man answering
Collins's description.

Inquiries will continue with a view of locating this
man.

D. Coffey

D. O. 38 G.

The Chief Comr.
Submitted
Bruton
Inspr for Supt 20/4/20

918
30·27 / Crime special

Very Secret

Michael Collins M.P.
South Cork.

County of Cork WR

Clonakilty 3/3/20

I beg to report that I
am reliably informed that
Michael Collins M.P. for south
Cork is permanently residing
in Dublin and is a constant
visitor at the residence of
John P. Twohig who is
employed in the Education
office. His private residence
is Craigmuller, Haddon road,
Clontarf and also at the
residence of Timothy Donovan,
Excise officer who resides at
3 St. Michaels, Sarsfield Road
Inchicore. These men are
married to two aunts of
Collins.

I was also told that Collins
walks the streets of Dublin
with two cousins of his
who are employed in the
The District

Communicated
Chief Commr 8/3/20

C.C. D.M.P.
Transmitted

a/ D.I.G.
8/3/1920

General Post office. Their names
are Hannah O'Brien and Mary
O'Brien but I do not know
where they stop in the City

M. Leary Head
53643

Clonakilty 3: 3: 20

Submitted.

H. Connor. 2nd DI

C1.

Bandon 4. 3. 20.

Submitted -

Collins' native place is Ardfield near
Clonakilty but he has not been there for a
long time now. If he stayed in that locality
the information would soon leak out as
he is well known there. The information
as to his being in Dublin is most probably
correct.

McGreen
for C1. onInsp.

1 G

FOR FURTHER READING

Béaslaí, Piaras. *Michael Collins and the Making of a New Ireland* (2 vols), Phoenix, 1926

Boyce, D.G. *Nationalism in Ireland*, Gill and Macmillan, 1982

Coogan, Tim Pat. *Michael Collins*, Hutchinson, 1990

Dwyer, T. Ryle. *Michael Collins*, Mercier Press, 1990

Forester, Margery. *Michael Collins: The Lost Leader*, Sidgwick and Jackson, 1971

Gaughan, J. Anthony. *Memoirs of Constable Jeremiah Mee, RIC*, Anvil Books, 1975

Herlihy, Jim. *The Royal Irish Constabulary: A Short History and Genealogical Guide*, Four Courts Press, 1997

Holt, Edgar. *Protest in Arms*, Putnam, 1960

Hopkinson, Michael. *Green Against Green*, Gill and Macmillan, 1988

'I.O.' [C.J.C. Street]. *The Administration of Ireland, 1920*, Philip Allan, 1921

Mackay, James. *Michael Collins: A Life*, Mainstream Publishing, 1996

Neligan, David. *The Spy in the Castle*, MacGibbon and Kee, 1968

Ó Broin, León. *Michael Collins*, Gill and Macmillan, 1980

O'Connor, Frank. *The Big Fellow*, Poolbeg, 1979

Taylor, Rex. *Michael Collins*, Hutchinson, 1958

INDEX